# VOTE OF CENSURE

GEORGE MALCOLM THOMSON

•

# VOTE
# OF
# CENSURE

•

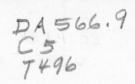

STEIN AND DAY/*Publishers*/New York

Printed in the United States of America

Stein and Day/*Publishers*/7 East 48 Street, New York, N.Y. 10017

*to*
*B.D.F.*

*Politics is the art of making possible that which is necessary.*

Paul Valéry

*At the summit, politics and strategy are one.*

Winston S. Churchill

# Contents

# List of Plates

# *Preface*

THE PERIOD BETWEEN JAPAN'S ENTRY into the
Second World War and Montgomery's victory in the
Battle of Alamein may reasonably be regarded as a dis-
tinct chapter in the history of the war, so far as Britain is
concerned. The events of that time were a test of the
Churchill Government's capacity to convince the public
that, in spite of setbacks and disasters, it deserved to survive in power. This it succeeded in doing, through eleven
months of intense political controversy, until victory in
the field brought the crisis to an end.

In this account of these events, I have naturally been
influenced by the angle from which I saw them—
rather close-up, somewhat to one side—as a member of
Lord Beaverbrook's personal staff at a time when he
was Minister of Supply and a member of the War
Cabinet.

But it is not simply due to this accident that Lord
Beaverbrook plays so large a part in the story. His relationship with Churchill was unique, his influence was, at
times, crucial. These two were the last two survivors of
Lloyd George's stormy but victorious government. They
were the paladins of 1918 who found themselves together
at the Cabinet table in 1940. Beaverbrook's influence over
the Prime Minister was, in my judgment, considerable
during those days. Behind it was an immense weight of
friendship, intelligence, shared experience and the cool,
crafty judgment with which one man corrected the imaginative genius of the other. It could not, in the nature of

things, be a decisive influence. It was in some quarters bitterly resented. But it was a steady, unobtrusive factor during critical weeks. Beaverbrook, it may be said, was the water in Churchill's wine.


I have been at some pains to compare and, if need be, correct my opinions on these events with the recollections of others who were actors or active spectators in the drama. In particular, I must mention with gratitude the help received from my close colleague of those days, Mr. David Farrer, whose critical and constructive zeal in overseeing the text would almost qualify him for the status of co-author, were it not that none of the book's defects can possibly be attributed to him.

I have also enjoyed frank exchanges about the time and its personalities with Lord Citrine, Lord Boothby, Sir Edmund Compton, Sir Hugh Weeks, Sir George Harvie-Watt, Sir Trevor Evans (whose recollections of the late Ernest Bevin were both piquant and helpful), Mr. Frank Owen, who guided my steps towards valuable sources of military enlightenment, Mr. William Barkley, Sir Alan Herbert, Mr. Kingsley Martin, Mr. Michael Foot, M.P., and Sir Dingle Foot, P.C., M.P., whose eye-witness account of the critical Commons debate of July 1942 supplied illuminating details. Mr. Tom Driberg, M.P., helped me with a graphic narrative of the Maldon by-election, which Sir Richard Acland supplemented from his own memories.

Mr. Emanuel Shinwell, P.C., C.H., M.P., opened to me his own vivid store of reminiscences of the time. So too did the late Sir John Wardlaw-Milne, a central figure in the Parliamentary story.

To all these gentlemen I owe a deep debt of gratitude. I should also acknowledge, although unhappily I cannot thank them, the benefits I derived in the past from discussion of these matters with the late Sir Archibald Rowlands and the late Mr. Arthur Christiansen.

Among the military figures of the time, I have drawn counsel and instruction from Field-Marshal Viscount Slim, Field-Marshal Lord Harding, Field-Marshal Sir Claude Auchinleck, General Sir Ian Jacob (who in particular has subjected my narrative of events in North Africa to sharp, well-informed criticism), Brigadier Sir John Smyth, BT., V.C., and from other distinguished soldiers who prefer to remain anonymous.

I ought to say that for all the military, as well as the political, judgments expressed I alone am responsible.

Through the kindness of Dorothy, Countess of Halifax, I have had the opportunity of examining her late husband's diaries at the City Library, York, where the staff were most helpful. I should mention here the kind assistance in this matter which I received from Major Tom Ingram.

Sir Basil Liddell Hart courteously allowed me to examine his invaluable archives relating to the war, and make use of unpublished material from them. I am grateful for these privileges, as I also am to the Franklin D. Roosevelt Library, Hyde Park, New York, for permission to quote from Lord Beaverbrook's letters to the President. Sir Max Aitken, BT., who has read the narrative, has kindly allowed me to quote from these letters of his father's.

I would like to say, too, with what gratitude I acknowledge my debt to the Gallup Poll, who have most kindly allowed me to quote from the wartime opinion polls of which they own the copyright and which are highly relevant to my purpose.

I must also thank my friend Mr. James McMillan for the helpful criticisms which he directed at the book while

it was being prepared. In particular, he persuaded me to
review my conclusion about some aspects of the war in
North Africa. Finally, let me say that from Miss Christine
Wallis I have drawn, throughout, collaboration beyond all
praise.

## CHAPTER I

# Porcupine Bank to Chesapeake Bay

*About 150 miles westward of Ireland there is an extensive bank, the shoalest part of which . . . is Porcupine bank, about 130 miles westward of Slyne head (Lat. 53° 24' N., Long. 10° 14' W.) . . .*
*Irish Coast Pilot*, 10th ed. (Hydrographic Department, Admiralty, 1954)

THE MAIDEN VOYAGE of H.M.S. *Duke of York* (battleship; 44,500 tons; armament: ten fourteen-inch guns in four turrets) was uncomfortable for the passengers, who numbered more than a hundred, because they were, for the most part, unused to being at sea in wartime conditions, and for the ship's company, numbering 1,800, because many of them had been compelled to give up their berths to the passengers. The weather in the Atlantic did nothing to make life more pleasant for either section during the crossing.

The Navy bore its unjust deprivations with exemplary stoicism and courtesy. The ratings, most of them boys from the Midlands at sea for the first time in the brand-new warship, suffered worst of all; they suffered in obscurity and silence. As for the passengers, civilian or service, they had many matters to distract their minds from the cold, the stiffness, the queasiness or—worse—the claustrophobia of life at sea, battened down under steel hatches, in a December gale. Some of them had important tasks; others felt that they were at least on the fringe of greatness.

Earlier that year, President Roosevelt had quoted Longfellow to Winston Churchill, who had quoted him to the British people:

> *Sail on, O Union strong and great,*
> *Thou, too, sail on, O Ship of State!*
> *Humanity with all its fears,*
> *With all the hopes of future years,*
> *Is hanging breathless on thy fate!*

The *Duke of York* might not in strict fact be the Ship of State but on that voyage it carried southwards and westwards into the storm some distinguished passengers: Mr. Winston Churchill, Prime Minister; Lord Beaverbrook, member of the War Cabinet and Minister of Supply; Mr. Averell Harriman, personal envoy of President Roosevelt; Sir Dudley Pound, First Sea Lord; Air-Marshal Sir Charles Portal, Chief of the Air Staff; Sir John Dill, lately Chief of the Imperial General Staff; and Sir Charles Wilson, Mr. Churchill's physician. The ministers and officials, with their immediate retinues of expert advisers, were faced by the need for rapid, concentrated and profound thought upon the problems and possibilities of the war which, in the previous few days, had changed in so spectacular a fashion.

Destiny was working to a tight schedule. On Sunday, 7 December, 1941, the American Pacific Fleet, attacked by Japanese aircraft at Pearl Harbour, had ceased to exist. One hour and twenty minutes earlier, Japanese troops of the 25th Army, "obeying the Emperor's august will for peace in the Far East",[1] landed at Kota Bharu in Malaya. But the full weight of the double blow was not, at first, apparent. Ten minutes before Lord Halifax, British Ambassador in Washington, was going out for his afternoon ride, a telephone call came from Roosevelt in the White House. He simply said: "The Japanese are bombing Hawaii; pass it on as quickly as you can to London." "So that's that," thought Halifax, and sent his horse back to the stable.[2]

The news had reached Lord Beaverbrook in the middle of dinner at Cherkley, his country house. He ordered a bottle of his best champagne from the cellar. "No. Make it two," he said. "We have just won the war."[3] One other man was of the same opinion. General de Gaulle said to Captain Billotte, "La guerre est finie. Bien sur, il y en aura encore pour des années, mais les Allemands sont battus."[4]

To Winston Churchill, the news came wearing a special air of deliverance and vindication. American entry into the war—in circumstances which could not be blamed on Britain's Machiavellian enticements—it was the triumph of his hopes, the confirmation of all he had laboured for. In August 1941 he had told Roosevelt during the Atlantic meeting that he would sooner have an American declaration of war and no supplies for six months than double supplies and no declaration.

Beyond that declaration, which in a few hours would be announced to the American Congress, Churchill's mind had never, it seems, effectively ventured. About the utterly transformed situation which it would inevitably bring he had given little, if any, thought. It was enough to know that all would be changed for the better: the war which could not plausibly be won had become the war which could not in the end be lost. In that knowledge, the setbacks and disappointments which were soon to come would be borne with fortitude.

The setbacks came, however, more swiftly and more severely than he had expected. Two days after Pearl Harbour, the British battleships, *Prince of Wales*, sister ship of the *Duke of York*, and *Repulse* were sunk by Japanese torpedo bombers off the coast of Malaya. Three days after that, Winston Churchill and his party boarded their train at Euston on the way to join the *Duke of York* at Greenock.

In a crisis so headlong and catastrophic, in which the two greatest naval powers had lost command of the sea over an area stretching, at the most optimistic view, over millions of square miles of ocean, no time was being lost by the head of one power to take counsel with the head of the other.

At Euston, the voyagers had been seen off by a cheerful gathering of their colleagues. The Prime Minister wore a blue boiler suit for the occasion. "The last time I saw the old gentleman in that," said one of Lord Beaverbrook's secretaries to another, "he was on the floor of Number 12 Downing Street with Lord Beaverbrook. They were playing with the model of a Churchill tank. Beaverbrook was angry because the model had to be pushed. He called me in. 'Get them to put a *clock* in the thing!' he said."

Sir Charles Craven of Vickers, with the long sardonic face of a comic actor, lifted a glass of *crème de menthe* in salute to a departing friend. "On the ship, look out for Y turret. It's not very good."

Averell Harriman, whose charming diffidence lent him a deceptive air of aloofness from the cares of less powerful mortals, arrived at the station in a swirl of fur and femininity—with his daughter Katherine and her friend Mrs. Randolph Churchill.

As the moment of departure approached, friends of the travellers began to make their way out of the train. Among them was Sir Archibald Rowlands, the great civil servant who was Permanent Secretary at the Ministry of Aircraft Production. He was unequalled in Whitehall in his capacity for work and unsurpassed in his power of mental concentration. He was, in the finest tradition of his service, completely dedicated to the public interest. He served that chilly mistress, the State, with the ardour of a saint who serves the Church. He had, in addition, gifts which are denied to most of the saints: a humorous affection for sinners, and an instinct for the moment when even the most sacred of rules may be broken.

He was short, dark, ruddy, Welsh of the Welsh. Between him and Lord Beaverbrook, who had been his Minister, existed a deep mutual regard which had survived early skirmishes. Moving from the train corridor to the platform, Rowlands winked in robust derision to a friend as he said his goodbyes.

A sergeant ran along the train carrying a respirator which might have been Churchill's. A sudden flourish of salutes. The train moved off into the darkness.

Next morning at Greenock, a grey sky, grey firth, grey hills behind it; in the foreground all the daunting energy of war. Merchant cruisers which had grown strange excrescences aft of the funnel. Flying boats. American destroyers with vivid light grey and pale blue camouflage. Countless lighters, patrol boats, trawlers, launches. Dominating the bustling scene, the *Duke of York*, on her deck a row of cheerful young officers commenting irreverently on the embarking passengers who, as they stepped gingerly aboard, were enfolded in the care of gigantic Royal Marines.

After no undue delay the ship began to move, in bleak foreboding sunlight, down the Clyde between two destroyers. The voyage was expected to last seven days, perhaps eight.

Churchill settled down in his cabin to prepare for the important and delicate task that lay ahead: his talks at Washington. He had been warned by Lord Halifax, the

British Ambassador to the United States, not to present too cut-and-dried a plan to the President, whose advisers must be allowed time to adjust themselves to the hurricane that had swept over their power in the Pacific and their policy in the world. At the same time, the British Prime Minister was resolved not to deny the Americans the benefit of his opinions and the experience of his chiefs in making war. Above all, he was intent on dissuading the Americans from putting the Pacific War ahead of the Western War in their planning.

Self-evident as this system of allocating priorities might seem to Churchill and his companions, it could by no means be assumed that the Americans shared their view. After all, it was in the Pacific and by the Japanese that the United States had been attacked. It could not be taken for granted that the mission on which the Prime Minister was hurrying with kindled enthusiasm and accumulated arguments would be an easy one to discharge.

Voyaging through the storm, south-west down the Irish Channel towards the Azores, across two streams of U-boats coming and going from the Biscay ports, dropping speed from twenty knots to seven, lest the *Duke of York's* destroyers be overwhelmed by the sea, Churchill journeyed to meet new anxieties. He had also, it must be said, left problems behind him.

On Monday, 15 December, the *Duke of York*, moving south by west towards the Azores, was somewhere off Porcupine Bank, about 200 miles from Galway Bay. Soon the ship would change course southwards. During the night, the gale had slowed the ship down to five knots, for fear that the attendant destroyers might go under. Meanwhile, 300 miles to the north, two convoys which had lost their escorts in the storm were at the mercy of U-boats.

Next day it seemed that the worst of the storm was over. The portholes were uncovered for the first time since leaving the Clyde. The ship made as much headway in twenty-four hours as in all the earlier days of the voyage. On the 17th, she was 300 miles from the Azores and due to pick up a new screen of destroyers. But it turned out that these were having fuel difficulties. So the decision was taken to go on alone, at speed.

Lord Beaverbrook, who looked with distaste on the expedition—the noise, the cold, the smell—and would have vastly preferred to fly, was pleased by the change of plan. He pointed out that for more than a day the *Duke of York* had been within 500 miles of Brest where there was a nest of long-range Focke Wulfs. These might have attacked and slowed the ship down, leaving her at the mercy of the U-boats.

Beaverbrook took little pleasure, either, in the evening entertainment aboard ship, for which the film unit of the Ministry of Information, knowing the Prime Minister's taste, had assembled a series of the most juvenile screen plays in the repertory. Over these nightly sessions the Prime Minister presided with droll delight, wearing a dressing-gown over his pyjamas which made him look like a monk belonging to some rather easy-going order. But the time was not wholly spent in amusement. The maps were inspected daily in their room: the ominous southward advance of the Japanese in Malaya was noted, the movements of convoys were followed, the demise of U-boats (off Bardia, off Cape St. Vincent) greeted with due satisfaction. When the storm returned, as it did on the 18th, the Met. Officer was summoned before the great to account for a gale he had failed to predict. By that time Churchill was becoming bored with the expedition, infected perhaps by the dogged melancholy of Lord Beaverbrook. Between the two Ministers there passed a flow of minutes,

half-serious, about certain inter-departmental disputes
they had left behind them in London.

The real business of the expedition was prepared in a
series of consultations which the Prime Minister held with
his advisers, Sir Dudley Pound, Chief of the Naval Staff,
Sir Charles Portal, Chief of the Air Staff, and Sir John
Dill, who had disagreed with Mr. Churchill over the relative importance of the Middle East and Singapore. The
Prime Minister, having decided that Sir John was "a tired
man", had replaced him as Chief of the Imperial General
Staff by Sir Alan Brooke. He was taking Dill to Washington and would leave him there.[5] The consultations on the
*Duke of York* bore fruit in three luminous minutes on the
part of the Prime Minister, which were to act as the foundations of the British case during the intense and far-
ranging discussions with the Americans which lay ahead.

Lord Beaverbrook, Minister of Supply, had his own
special duty, the congenial one of convincing the United
States that it really *was* an industrial power greater by far
than any on earth. The task was one for which by temperament, experience, background and gifts he was eminently suited.

In that strange nautical interlude at the supreme crisis
of the war, the strategic brain of Britain worked at high
pressure in an over-crowded, uncomfortable, storm-
battered vessel in the mid-Atlantic.

The Foreign Secretary, Mr. Anthony Eden, arrived in
Moscow about the time the Prime Minister and his reti-
nue left Greenock. Eden's task was to smooth Stalin down
and, if possible, to reach an understanding with him.
Meanwhile, the Lord Privy Seal, Mr. Attlee and the resi-
due of the Ministry kept the business of government in
motion in London. The acting Prime Minister can hardly
have doubted that public opinion in Britain was in a
restive mood—and likely to grow more so.

About five o'clock in the afternoon of Sunday, 21
December, the *Duke of York* picked up her screen of
American destroyers, unfamiliar silhouettes on which the
Royal Navy cast a disapproving eye: "Ugly boats". Two
days and two bad films later, the ship dropped anchor in
Chesapeake Bay—Royal Marines drawn up on the
quarterdeck, salutes, "Rule Britannia".

The Prime Minister and his attendant grandees left by
aeroplane to dine at the White House. The lesser figures
were landed by launch at Fort Monroe at half past five
and, some hours later, left the deserted railway station of
Phoebus for Washington, which they reached at two
o'clock in the morning. The weather was cold in the city;
a frost was coming.

Thus the "Arcadians", so called after the code-name
of the expedition, arrived in the city which fifteen days
earlier had become the most important capital in the
world.

## CHAPTER II
# Lion in a den of Daniels

*When the ministry was offered him, he put on all the appearance of a man who dreaded its labours and difficulties. They had almost to resort to violence to make him accept the power which he was burning to possess.*
    —Etienne Pasquier on Chateaubriand

CHURCHILL TOOK WITH HIM on that momentous voyage the second most powerful and by far the most contentious figure in the Government: Lord Beaverbrook, the Canadian press-lord who, at the Ministry of Aircraft Production, had maintained the flow of fighters that won the Battle of Britain and was, at that moment, Minister of Supply.

Churchill's ministers had diverse qualities and were chosen for diverse reasons. Clement Attlee, leader of the Labour Party, was a man with a genius for self-effacement, whom nobody knew well and whom many people despised. He had still to disclose the capacity for crisp decision that later made him formidable. Herbert Morrison, Home Secretary, was the most able political organizer of his time. Ernest Bevin, Minister of Labour, was a burly and fearless trade union leader whose egotism was so total and unconscious that it was almost sublime. "Between a spoilt child and a bear with a sore head," said Lord Halifax—who later changed his opinion. Apparently devoid of logical processes, he had flair instead—flair and staying power. Detesting Herbert Morrison from the bottom of his heart, he had in recent months found a new object for his suspicion and dislike: Beaverbrook.

Churchill's ministers were a band of brothers and, as brothers will, they quarrelled with, distrusted and black-guarded one another. None roused more animosity among the others than Beaverbrook, who was capable of giving as good as he got. In many ways Beaverbrook was the most unexpected face in that ministerial gallery.

It was more than thirty years since Beaverbrook (then Max Aitken), whose business career in Canada was over by the age of thirty, crowned with a spectacular success, had left his native land for Britain. To go on piling up money by further commercial adventures was repugnant to one of his essentially economical nature. It would be a manifest waste of effort, ability and spirit. Besides, he had been brought up in the stimulating and intensely political atmosphere of a Presbyterian manse. Public life made an irresistible appeal. At this moment, the old country shone before him as the land of promise and opportunity. It was at the same time known—to a young man steeped in its history—and unknown. It was old, complex and fascinating, arrogant and hospitable, an oyster eager to be opened. He left Canada and settled in Britain.

That London was curious about the wealthy young immigrant from Montreal can be assumed. What is not to be overlooked is the avid curiosity, oddly compounded of veneration and impatience, with which he approached London society and British political life in the last weeks of the reign of Edward VII.

One day in 1911, at a hospitable dinner table, he heard Winston Churchill, the brilliant, irresponsible member of Mr. Asquith's Cabinet, hold forth to the company. The

young Canadian millionaire was spellbound by such
exuberance of spirit, fertility of ideas and profusion of
language. Turning to his neighbour, he exclaimed in enthusiasm: "Ah, I would give five pounds to have that man
at my dinner table." "Done!" cried his neighbour who,
as it chanced, was F. E. Smith, later first Lord Birkenhead, one of Churchill's closest personal friends and
fiercest political foes.

From that day onwards the two men saw a great deal of
one another, in spite of the fact that Aitken became the
political lieutenant of Bonar Law, whose distrust of
Churchill was unsleeping and whom Churchill despised.
They had been together in London on the eve of the First
World War. When Churchill left Admiralty House to slip
across the Horse Guards Parade to Number Ten and tell
Asquith that he was going to mobilize the Fleet, it was
Aitken whom he asked to take his hand at bridge.

When Churchill was cast out of the Government after
the Dardanelles affair, it was to Beaverbrook's country
house at Cherkley that he repaired for solace. There he
proposed to seek oblivion in art. Putting up his easel and
setting out his colours on the palette, he had settled down
to paint the scene when he remembered that, after all, he
owed some entertainment to his host. "As for you, Max,"
he said, "I have brought something that will occupy your
mind." And he placed on Lord Beaverbrook's table a
massive pile of documents, the evidence given to the
Dardanelles Commission.

Through good fortune and ill, the rare agreements, the
frequent disputes, friendship between the two men persisted. It was based upon a deep enjoyment by each of the
other as a human being of rich, if eccentric, quality.
Churchill's affection was streaked with wariness, Beaverbrook's contained a canny disapproval of Churchill's
romantic impressionism, in politics as in painting.

The relationship was fed by memories of bygone crises, frolics and persons, which, as time passed, fewer and fewer men could share with them. Memories, for instance, of the wonderful swashbuckling Birkenhead, central figure of a set of gay, wild, rich—or extravagant—young men.

When every other subject of reminiscence dried up between the two, they could always fall back upon an inexhaustible source of exasperation and amusement—the subtlety and adroitness of the great Lloyd George. Each of them bore the scars of wounds inflicted by that dazzling and darting warrior.

One day in 1916, at a time when Lloyd George was forming his Government, he was dining at F. E. Smith's in the company of Churchill and Beaverbrook. When dinner was over, Lloyd George asked Beaverbrook to drive along with him. Beaverbrook thought that his hour had arrived: he was about to be offered a ministry. But all Lloyd George said was simply: "Go back and tell Winston his time has not yet come."

Returning to Smith's dinner table, Beaverbrook sought to steer the conversation so that he could deliver this message to Churchill, who was in an exultant, teasing mood. What office, he wondered, would the Prime Minister bestow on Beaverbrook? "Oh, probably none at all," said Beaverbrook sombrely. 'Oh, come, come," said Churchill, carrying on the joke, "surely he will at least make you Postmaster-General."

In his annoyance at this barb, Beaverbrook used a phrase which indicated to Churchill that neither of them was going to be given office. Churchill rose in a rage. "Smith," he cried, "*this man knows*!" Taking up his cane and his coat, he left the house abruptly. Later—and characteristically—he apologized for having made such a scene.

When, in due and unhurried course, Lloyd George defied the displeasure of Bonar Law and appointed Churchill Minister of Munitions, Beaverbrook was used as the messenger who carried the bad news to Bonar Law but, to his chagrin, was still given no post himself.

Churchill made a kindly offer to the disappointed man. "You can be my Under-Secretary."

Beaverbrook shook his head: "I should be delighted. But I am still on the black list."

Between the wars, the two men, so different in outlook yet drawn together by so powerful a magnet of mutual curiosity and liking, kept alive the flame of friendship. Apart from anything else, they shared some antipathies. They knew that, in a political era weak in colour, they at least were exceptional men. Laughter came sometimes to cement the companionship.

One day in the summer of 1929, Beaverbrook had taken a party of friends in his yacht over to Belgium. Churchill, who had been Chancellor of the Exchequer in Baldwin's Government, until a general election brought the Labour Party into power, was among them. Going ashore, they made their way to Antwerp, where a popular demonstration of some sort was in progress. They joined in the procession and were carried along with it to the centre of the city.

Suddenly, Churchill was alarmed by some of the songs chanted by their fellow-marchers. The sentiments were not at all to his liking. There seemed to be a great many red flags in evidence. After making enquiry, he left the procession abruptly.

In the United States two anarchists, Sacco and Vanzetti, had been sentenced to death for the murder of a paymaster and the theft of 3,750 dollars. The two men, who were then widely believed to be innocent, became heroes and martyrs of the proletariat all over the world. A vast agitation to demand their reprieve spread through the industrial centres of Europe and America.

Churchill, former Chancellor of the Exchequer, known for his dislike of the revolutionary movement, had saved himself in time from innocent participation in a Sacco-Vanzetti demonstration. The humour of this occasion was not lost either on him or on Beaverbrook. It was one of the less important of the memories they shared.

Between the wars, however, something more important than common memories came to divide them. The old quarrel over Bonar Law was succeeded by a new and far more serious quarrel over the policy to be followed towards the new Germany which Hitler brought into being. It divided two men who were no longer the careless, angry young politicians of 1911. Each was graver, although each was saved from conformity by an unconquerable quirk of temperament.

Beaverbrook was a man exceptionally well informed about foreign affairs through a wide range of personal meetings with eminent Europeans over the years: Germans like Walter Rathenau (who made the mistake of trying to bribe him), Stresemann ("I will not live to see the Second Punic War, but my children will"), Richard von Kühlmann, whom he liked, and Ribbentrop, whom he regarded as a bad joke; all the Frenchmen in public life from Clemenceau onwards; any Russian who would talk; any Italian who would talk sense. They talked freely to the best listener in Europe.

He had no illusions at all about the men who had clambered into the saddle in Germany. He had been told by the Egyptian Ambassador in London, fresh from Nazi Berlin: "They are gangsters in command of a great nation." He had visited Berlin and found no reason to alter that verdict.

Goering had repeated to him words that he had uttered

not long before at the window of his hotel room, while watching a Nazi parade. In the room a microphone had been concealed.

He had gone to Berlin for the Olympic Games, had admired the showmanship and, through no initiative of his own, had met Hitler. The *Führer* had failed to impress him, had failed to rouse in him even that spark of amused appreciation which Mussolini had kindled.

The gloomy session in Berlin had been overhung with mutual antipathy. But dislike of Hitler the man did not convince Beaverbrook that war with him was necessary; it was certainly not desirable in his opinion. Churchill's conviction was otherwise: believing that the ancient war-like spirit of the Germans was on the march again in Europe, his aim was to exorcise it by arms, and the sooner the better.

As early as October 1933, at a time of international crisis, he was speaking to Beaverbrook in those terms. Beaverbrook objected: the Dominions would not march. "Don't be too sure, Max," said Churchill. "Your predictions do not always come true."

At that moment, Beaverbrook's memory performed one of its periodic miracles.

"Do you remember," he said, "a conversation with me in July 1914? It was on the 17th. We went for a walk and talked about the war that was coming. You doubted if the Dominions would come in. I said I was sure they would. And you said: 'Don't be too sure, Max'."

Sir Samuel Hoare (later Lord Templewood), when he was a member of Chamberlain's Cabinet, had kept Beaverbrook in touch almost every week with the thoughts of the British Government on the European situation. In an earlier stage, Sir Robert Vansittart (later Lord Vansittart) permanent head of the Foreign Office, had seen a great deal of Beaverbrook without influencing in the least his inflexible policy of detachment from Europe.

In 1932 the British Government had advanced £4,500,000 to Austria in an attempt to bolster it up against pressure from Germany. This loan was strongly criticized in the *Daily Express*. Later, in 1933, the Italian ambassador, Count Grandi, told Vansittart that Britain should do more to help Austria.

Vansittart replied: "Impossible. Lord Beaverbrook made such a row about the four and a half million pounds that we cannot do any more. Max is a very ignorant and mischievous man but very clever, with a remarkable gift of putting his point of view in a vulgar way. . . . It is impossible to flatter him. He is too vain."

Grandi and Ivan Maisky, the Russian, were latterly the two ambassadors in whose company Beaverbrook took most pleasure, until the day came when it was no longer suitable for a man in his position, in control of powerful newspapers, to have social relations with the representatives of certain foreign states.

As the thirties advanced and the crisis in Europe grew more acute, Beaverbrook was, very soon, in trouble over two contributors to his newspaper the *Evening Standard*: David Low, the cartoonist, and Winston Churchill, who wrote regularly in the newspaper, usually on the single theme of the danger threatening Britain from Hitler. There were variations, but the theme was dominant, recurrent and unmistakable. It was irritating to the British Government, at that time engaged on its ill-fated attempt to buy peace with Hitler; it was resented in Germany.

Beaverbrook found that one of his newspaper properties had become, through the activity of a powerful and persistent advocate, a resounding instrument of propaganda against the policy in which he himself believed. He was correspondingly annoyed.

After unavailing attempts had been made to divert

Churchill from his favourite subject, the editor of the *Evening Standard*, Percy Cudlipp, decided to get rid of the embarrassing journalist. Churchill was not for a moment in doubt about whose hand had really struck the blow He disappeared from the pages of the *Evening Standard* in April 1938, not without grief; for his articles, syndicated throughout the world, owed some of their prestige to the fact that they first appeared in Lord Beaverbrook's newspaper.

As for Low, the Nazi campaign against him, which did not lack ingenuity, reached its climax after Lord Halifax paid a visit to the Hunting Exhibition in Berlin. He passed on to Low Dr. Goebbels' thesis that the Germans regarded their *Führer* more or less as the British regarded their King, as one above the vulgar comments of cartoonists and the like. Low was not convinced by this revelation. His cartoons in the *Evening Standard* continued to annoy Goebbels and, if he was allowed to see them, Hitler. Churchill, on the other hand, was driven to find a new pulpit, which he did without any difficulty. His expulsion from the columns of the *Evening Standard* marked a low point in his relations with Beaverbrook.

All this lay buried deep under the avalanche of war, when Churchill made Lord Beaverbrook his Minister of Aircraft Production in 1940. It would, of course, be absurd to suggest that the reason for Churchill's choice of the Minister was anything so insubstantial as a desire to have somebody at the Cabinet table to whom he could talk about old times. He had formed over the years a profound admiration for Beaverbrook as a companion-in-arms with a quicksilver and sinewy resourcefulness.

In how many political scrapes had Beaverbrook given events the new twist that saved—or transfixed—a Minister! In how many personal dramas had he intervened to stifle a scandal or save a name! Never having any need himself to fear embarrassments of that kind, Churchill was all the more impressed when he heard of Max's ingenious rescue operations on behalf of others.

He remembered how, in 1922, when the Tory Party was about to make up its mind between continuing in the Coalition under Lloyd George or resuming an independent existence under Bonar Law, a by-election at Cardiff was held to be of critical importance. An independent Conservative was standing against a Coalition candidate. Until that result was known, the fateful meeting at the Carlton Club was postponed. Hearing that the Coalition candidate was doing badly, Beaverbrook, forceful ally of Bonar Law, made a flying visit to the constituency, a few days before the poll, taking with him ample sinews of war. The Coalition candidate was beaten, with a corresponding influence in depressing the Coalition cause in Parliament. In the Carlton Club meeting that followed immediately afterwards, Bonar Law found himself an astounded victor and the new Prime Minister.

In another, and very different incident, widely known at the time, Beaverbrook's quick-wittedness was his own salvation. During the war, at a time when Beaverbrook was already a peer and when he still supervised the Canadian War Records Office in Lombard Street in the City, he was visited one day by a man named Robertson Lawson, an accountant who was the head of Liptons' Stores. Robertson Lawson pointed a revolver at Beaverbrook announcing: "I have been sent here on a mission. Either you are good, in which case the Holy Ghost will come down and settle on you, or you are evil and I will destroy you."

Beaverbrook realized the appalling truth: Robertson Lawson had gone mad. In so tragic an emergency, he had one idea: to play for time in the hope that something, or somebody, would turn up. He tried all sorts of arguments on the lunatic. They sang together two Psalms, the 23rd and the 109th, from the Scottish Psalter. He rattled off all the prayers he could remember from boyhood days in the manse at Newcastle, New Brunswick, where he was brought up.

Robertson Lawson brought him sternly to a sense of the proprieties.

"On your knees, Beaverbrook," he cried. Down went Lord Beaverbrook on the carpet.

In spite of all these devices, Robertson Lawson seemed to be more and more convinced that Beaverbrook was evil and ought to be destroyed. Beaverbrook resisted this logic, saying that he was sure the Holy Ghost had already arrived. Robertson Lawson rejected this opinion. The Holy Ghost would come in the form of a dove; he could see no dove.

At that point, Beaverbrook, whose mind always worked best in moments of danger, had a fresh idea. "In this building," he pointed out, "there are many wicked people whose presence will inevitably prevent the entry of the Holy Ghost. It will be quite different in a consecrated building."

The argument appealed to Robertson Lawson as eminently reasonable. The two men set off together to find a church. Along the corridor. Into a crowded lift. Beaverbrook remained silent. The revolver was in Robertson Lawson's pocket, pointed at him.

In the street outside, there was a great deal of traffic. Beaverbrook plunged into it, losing his hat in the process, and ran as fast as he could to a police station. He gave his name and told what was happening. Only half believing, the police allowed him to use their telephone.

After failing to find Bonar Law, he got through to a friend, who sent a car to fetch him. At the same time, he sent a warning note to Sir Robert Donald, editor of the

*Daily Chronicle*, that Robertson Lawson meant to kill him too. Donald made off at once to Walton Heath.

When the car arrived, Beaverbrook told the police that the madman might be lurking outside; they must protect him. They did. He arrived safely at a friend's house, where he found Bonar Law and F. E. Smith. After telling them what had happened, he left for his house in the country, somewhat shaken by events.

Robertson Lawson's wife telephoned there to say that her husband had come home and threatened to kill her. When she took refuge in a pantry, he had forced the door and broken her arm. Then the police arrived and took him to a padded cell, where he died three days later. Mrs. Robertson Lawson asked Lord Beaverbrook to be a pall-bearer at the funeral. This honour he declined.

In the meantime, F. E. Smith had carried the story to Westminster, where it was received with delight. Indeed, Smith and Augustine Birrell, the former Chief Secretary for Ireland, developed it into a dramatic performance in which Smith took the part of Robertson Lawson and Birrell was Beaverbrook. They sang and prayed, and the climax came when Smith shouted "On your knees, Beaverbrook" and Birrell got down on the floor.

It was some time before Beaverbrook saw the full comedy of an episode which, in fact, had reflected enormous credit on his coolness and cunning.

These were among the qualities which Churchill had discerned in his friend and which he sought to harness when he brought Beaverbrook into his Cabinet.

Beaverbrook had not believed that it was necessary to fight the war. As far as one patriotic man could, he had opposed Britain's involvement. Trusting Chamberlain's resolve to keep Britain out (of which he had received

private assurances that seemed to be reliable) he had predicted almost up to the last year of peace that there would
be no war in Europe.

Thus when, in spite of all his hopes and beliefs, war did
break out in September 1939, Beaverbrook suffered a
double blow. He was hurt in his pride as a publicist and
also in his common sense as a human being. He was outraged by the gigantic waste that he foresaw and, it may
be, annoyed by the arrival on the scene of a power more
imperious and commanding than even the richest and
most influential of magnates: war.

Whatever the issue of the war might be, however long
or short the duration of the cyclone, it was bound to
sweep bare whole regions of established wealth and grace
and tolerance. It must make vast changes in the order on
which the world rested. He could not see how any good
could come commensurate with the suffering and destruction that lay ahead.

So this proud and pugnacious man was willing to be
called an "appeaser" and to number himself with mild
men like Chamberlain, Hoare and Halifax. It was an
ironic choice. For Beaverbrook was a fighting man of the
most distinguished vehemence, at once vengeful and mag-
nanimous, a figure with some of Balzac's qualities, the
Balzac who said, "My critics want to scalp me and *I want
to drink out of their skulls.*"

Whatever else Beaverbrook was, mild he was not!

When Harold Laski met him, he said: "I can't understand, Lord Beaverbrook, how you, disapproving as you
do of the hereditary principle, ever accepted a peerage."

Beaverbrook made some vague answer—times change,
circumstances alter, etc. Then, with more emphasis, he
went on: "But I'll tell you one thing, Laski. When I went
into that gilded chamber for the first time, I felt like a lion
going into a den of Daniels."[1]

This lion had, in truth, a dual and stormy nature, in which seams of generous impulse ran through a basic layer of caution. When generosity had won, as it usually did, the matter was not over, for at once he would accuse himself of having given way to weakness. So he seemed to be carrying on an incessant debate with himself or rather between two levels of his mind which were, at the same time, moving in opposite directions. He was supremely a man of action but one of a special kind, an intellectual, whose action proceeded from a gift of rapid, crude analysis, tearing away the inessentials of a problem and laying bare the beating heart.

He had, too, the power of imposing his interests or decisions on others as if they were moral duties. He was capable of exhibitions of volcanic anger convincing and daunting to everyone save the physician who took his pulse before and after those outbursts and found that it was not altered. Yet, while the storm lasted, he seemed to draw a just indignation from some private well of divine wrath, independent of the rights and wrongs of the case, whatever it might be. The gift, which had served him in the market-place, was deployed in the business of government.

During the mission to Washington, one of his assistants was asked to provide him with some figures of rubber stocks. The assistant had three agencies to choose from as the source of the information, and chose the wrong one. There was a crisis, in the course of which the erring assistant was summoned to see Lord Beaverbrook.

"Well, how did you get on?" asked a colleague afterwards.

"Oh, the Minister was very nice. He gave me some brandy."

"Brandy?"

"Well, of course, I fainted."

Yet to emphasize, as he was apt to do, the roughness of his character at the expense of his other gifts would be to fall into a pit which he himself has dug. He took a perverse pleasure in misrepresenting himself, perhaps because he wished to lay stress upon qualities which he only half possessed and which told only half the story of himself. Subtlety, not crudity, was the secret of his being. Those who saw him in the public arena saw only the strident showman who seemed to delight in the dust, having already gathered in a full sheaf of the palms. Those who looked a little closer did not always like what they saw. To men like Sir James Grigg—Permanent Secretary at the War Office, later Secretary of State for War—and Sir Stafford Cripps, he was Anti-Christ, Churchill's evil genius, a Mephistophelian figure of infinite mischief. Some of this dislike for him he had impishly provoked, and some he had earned.

On the other hand, he had the capacity for winning the admiration of men who did not give their praise easily—men like Sir Archibald Rowlands—and the deep and lasting love of beautiful, intelligent and sensitive women. This must be mentioned because it suggests something that is true: Beaverbrook was a man of far more complex temperament than most of his contemporaries in public affairs. He touched life at many more points than they did. Even Churchill was composed of simpler strands, although the cloth was woven on an ampler loom.

There are three well-defined types of political leader: the warrior (Churchill), the prophet (Hitler or de Gaulle) and the thaumaturge or magician (Franklin Roosevelt and Lloyd George), about whose figure there clings an uncanny light that never shone on land or sea. Beaverbrook belonged to this third type. He entered into legend before he took his place in history, and the legend was half at least of his own inventing.

Thus it was not enough for him that his achievement in meeting the aircraft supply emergency in the summer of 1940 should be—as it certainly was—a triumph of improvisation, dynamic leadership, energy and harsh realism. It was a truly extraordinary performance, a historic enterprise in national salvation. But to satisfy Beaverbrook's pride in what he had done, it was necessary for him to add a spark of the miraculous, so that he seemed to conjure aircraft out of nothing and hurl them into the empty sky.

He had thought that Britain should avoid the war, on the simple strategic principle that one ought not to jump into the ring at the moment when the antagonist is spoiling for a fight. One delays, dissembles and waits until the foe is occupied in another quarter. In national matters, as in the smaller feuds of journalism, Beaverbrook believed in the strategy of indirect approach—unexpected reprisal.

Lion or no lion, Beaverbrook's intellectual rejection of the war persisted for some time after the conflict had begun.

Whether in fact Britain could advantageously have postponed war in 1939 may be doubted. She would have been required to make a stupendous effort in rearmament in time of peace against the danger of a war which, her leaders would be bound to insist, was receding! A democracy, especially the British democracy, needs the spur of danger. But Beaverbrook went on hoping that, after the destruction of Poland, some method could be found of stamping out the flames before, with a change of wind, they spread to the West.

It was not like him to remain a passive worshipper at the shrine of hope, and in the period known as "the phoney war" he took some interest in quasi-pacifist activities which later on, when the world had changed, became a source of embarrassment to him.

As the story is told by Mr. John McGovern, a member of the Independent Labour Party and at that time M.P. for Shettleston, he, along with Mr. James Maxton, M.P., and Mr. Campbell Stephen, M.P., were approached by Mr. W. J. Brown, a trade union leader, a few months after the outbreak of war. Brown told them that Lord Beaverbrook would be glad of a talk with them. They saw him at Stornoway House, his own house in St. James's. Beaverbrook then suggested that, if they put up "peace candidates" at by-elections, he would provide £500 for each seat they fought and see that their meetings were well reported in his newspapers. Nothing came of the idea.

When McGovern and Maxton next visited Stornoway House, France was about to fall and Beaverbrook had become a member of Churchill's Government. He had, in fact, that very day returned from Tours, where he had heard Churchill's historic and moving appeal to the French Government to fight on. Plainly there could no longer be any question of "peace candidates". Britain was fighting for her life and Beaverbrook had thrown himself into the fight. There was no inconsistency between this action and his earlier doubts about the wisdom of the war. It may be said that it was when Hitler invaded Norway and Denmark that Beaverbrook declared war.

A few weeks later, on a Sunday morning, McGovern told a private study circle in Glasgow about the by-election proposal. The story did not, however, remain within the study circle.

In 1941 a by-election took place in Greenock, a constituency held by the Labour Party and defended on their behalf by Mr. Hector McNeil against a Communist challenger, Gunner Bob Cooney. Cooney called off the fight at the last minute, on 9 July, because, a few days before, Hitler had attacked Russia and, by doing so, put into reverse the views about the war of every Communist

in the world. Before his conversion, however, Gunner
Cooney had published in an election sheet an account of
what McGovern had told the study circle about Lord
Beaverbrook's by-election suggestion.

The matter was raised at question time in the House of
Commons, where it caused a considerable hullabaloo.
When Churchill said he was assured that the statements
were untrue Maxton interjected that, if it were to become
a matter of public controversy, Mr. McGovern's word
would not go unsupported. Feeling that his reputation
was besmirched, McGovern wrote on 12 July to Beaverbrook, recalling the by-election offer. He could not deny
the Communist story, he said, because it was true.

Meetings in London followed between the parties to
the dispute, all of whom were united by a desire to bring
the embarrassing business somehow to an end. At one
meeting Beaverbrook said jokingly to Maxton: "All
right, Jimmy, I admit that I was the agitator. I have always
been an agitator." This, at least, is McGovern's recollection of the incident.

In the end, he decided to pursue the matter no further.
Beaverbrook sent him a private letter with authority to
make use of it were he challenged in an election. The letter
(29 July, 1941) contained the sentence, "If I do not
accept your recollections, I do not doubt your integrity."[2]
Thus to the relief of all, ended a little comedy which a
later age may find puzzling and which has little interest
now save to illustrate the sudden veerings of opinion and
the strained atmosphere characteristic of those early
months of war.

Beaverbrook had become a leading statesman in a
struggle the origins of which were, for him, clouded by
error. But once the issue was irrevocable he did not look
back. For instance, he was never for a moment tempted
by the "peace offers" which Hitler dangled before the

British Government through the King of Sweden and other agents. It was no time for parley, he said.

Even so, he carried into his role of man of action some vestiges of 1939. Behind the blare of the martial trumpets could at times be heard inconvenient echoes of a gentler music from the past.

And he was not, at any time, psychologically involved in the war to the degree that Churchill was, or Ernest Bevin (outraged by Hitler's ill-treatment of German trade union leaders) or Anthony Eden, Mussolini's victim, symbol for pre-war youth of the anti-Fascist spirit, or Cripps, round whom could be heard the distant echoes of "Arms for Spain".

A certain intellectual coolness distinguished Beaverbrook's approach to the struggle from that of most of his colleagues in Churchill's Government. He was drawn more and more into its problems and excitements, but these remained incidents in a fascinating and cruel game, rather than a crusade. This element of intellectual detachment helped him to be critical at times of Churchill's strategy and to develop an independent line of thought. Thus, without difficulty, the man who would have been willing, in 1939, to acquiesce in a German onslaught on Russia became, two years later, an enthusiastic supporter of the Second Front. Such changes of course are easier to a man whose basic sympathies are not engaged.

When Churchill flew to Tours on 13 June, 1940, he took with him Halifax, at that time Foreign Secretary, and Beaverbrook, who a month earlier had become Minister for Aircraft Production and on whom the Prime Minister knew he could count for immediate, wise advice in moments of crisis.

As Beaverbrook could not disclose the nature of his

journey to any of his staff, his valet, Nockels, packed for a week-end. In the hall of Stornoway House an odd little scene was enacted on the morning of departure.

Beaverbrook and two valets knelt side by side on the marble floor and threw unwanted clothes out of his suit-cases. While this was going on, the door-bell rang and a stately gentleman was disclosed who, to an audience of bottoms, launched into a speech expressing the admira-tion Queen Mary felt about some recent articles in the *Daily Express*. He was the Queen's equerry.

After Beaverbrook had dismissed the emissary with some courteous words, he found he had no money for the journey. He raised ten pounds from his Civil Service secretary (now Sir Edmund Compton, "Ombudsman"), five pounds from the chauffeur and seven pounds ten shillings from miscellaneous sources. Then he drove off to Admiralty House where the Prime Minister was wait-ing. The journey from Whitehall to Hendon airfield was completed in exactly seventeen minutes.

Then followed Tours, the scenes and the visages of *débâcle*, Churchill's final appeal to the French Cabinet (which Beaverbrook, who heard it, considered the most impressive of all his speeches), the adjournment to the garden of the Prefecture, the puddles and the wet sunlit leaves of the laurel-bushes, and Beaverbrook's abrupt summing-up in a harsh voice that admitted no argument: "We are doing no good here. . . . Let's get along home." [3]

When they returned to Hendon that night, after the historic and harrowing day, the pilot of the aircraft asked Churchill if he had found the trip uncomfortable. "I did not notice anything," replied the Prime Minister. "I slept all the way." Then, stretching his arms, he said to his companions, "Well, we'll meet at ten," meaning that there would be a Cabinet at that hour. (It was then about nine.)

Lord Halifax protested: they had been at it all day and they were very tired.

"All right," said Churchill, "make it ten-fifteen."

"There was," as he says in his history, "a long way to go before bed-time."[4]

Beaverbrook, moved and shaken by the experience, said on reaching his house: "I have seen immense events."

They were, as it proved, only the prelude to events still more immense: the Battle of Britain, and a mission to Washington in the summer of 1941, immediately after the Atlantic Charter meeting, when he laid the foundations of his friendship with Franklin D. Roosevelt. A few weeks later came a journey even more momentous. Beaverbrook went to Moscow with Averell Harriman on a supply mission which was also a reconnaissance. Behind the overt question, "What arms does Russia need that we can furnish?", lay the hidden one, "Will Russia stay in the war?" On that visit Beaverbrook made a friend of Stalin and an enemy of Sir Stafford Cripps, the Socialist politician who was at that time British Ambassador in Moscow.

Beaverbrook's probe into the Kremlin was, rightly, judged to be a diplomatic triumph. In the more genial but hardly less Byzantine atmosphere of the White House, an equally important task now awaited him.

# CHAPTER III

# The Christmas tree on the White House lawn

*Speak of next year and the Devil laughs.*
—Japanese proverb

THE BRITISH EXPEDITION TO WASHINGTON in the last month of 1941 brought to that city, still astounded and sobered to find itself at war, a somewhat battered expertise in military affairs which, with the best will in the world on both sides, was liable to become irritating. It is hard for the most tactful of veterans to prevent a faint insufferable nuance of patronage fron insinuating itself, unawares, into the advice which he presses on the soldier newly arrived on the battlefield. But the role of war-scarred counsellor was not the only one that President Roosevelt's British guests were hoping to assume.

Santa Claus was arriving just in time for Christmas, his sack swollen with hard-won advice and little else. More than that, he intended to reverse the traditional order of things and depart better off than he had come. On the White House lawn the President's Christmas tree might not yet be lighted, but already, in the imagination of his British guests, its branches glittered with gifts appropriate to the year if not to the season—tanks, guns, fighters, bombers, warships—the fruits of America's arsenals, and now, surely, about to equip America's allies as well as her own armies. The need for such a reinforcement was desperate.

Britain, having entered the war with an inadequate stock of weapons, had lost, at Dunkirk, the equivalent of eight to ten months' output of her arms factories.

This seems a reasonable deduction from a note which Churchill sent to General Ismay on 2 June, 1940.[1] "Our losses in equipment must be expected to delay the fruition of our expansion of the B.E.F. from the twenty divisions formerly aimed at by Z [i.e. outbreak of war] +12 months to no more than fifteen divisions by Z+18." Six months longer; five divisions fewer.

The losses at Dunkirk included 700 tanks, 2,500 guns (1,200 field and bigger guns; 1,300 anti-aircraft and anti-tank guns) and 120,000 vehicles. At that time production, although mounting steadily, was running at a monthly rate of 42 field guns, 136 large anti-aircraft guns, 303 two-pounder and Bofors guns and 115 tanks.[2] The equipment lost in Greece and Crete, a year later, was equal to that of four and a half divisions and included 8,000 vehicles.

By that time, however, supplies were flowing more amply and losses could be made good more swiftly.

Thus, as a result of a succession of strategical misfortunes, Britain had not been able to translate the output of her factories into a proportionate net increment to armed strength in the field. She had suffered more than the normal wastage of war.

There was, too, a weakness inherent in the whole conception of an active war in the Middle East.

When the collapse of France occurred in the summer of 1940, Churchill's riposte had been spirited and audacious. He had reinforced Egypt with armour. This action had paid precious dividends in sustaining national morale during a period of grim discouragement. It might, with cooler judgment, have brought far-reaching military rewards. As it was, Rommel arrived in Africa and the campaign in the desert bogged down in frustration. Its balance-sheet began to move into the red.

It was justified as a traditional use of British sea power against a continental enemy enjoying a vast superiority on land. The illustrious example of the Peninsular War was invoked. The theory was that the command of the sea enables the power with the superior navy to bring about a dispersal of the enemy's forces and then attack him at some point on his extended coast line where his reply would be difficult and expensive. The classic statement of the doctrine was given to the world by the American Admiral Alfred Thayer Mahan: "In the history of the world sea-power has always decided the destiny of nations." However, this principle could be applied only with severe reservations to a war in the Middle East.

To keep aircraft in the air over the desert, 1,000 men worked in one assembly depot alone, at Port Sudan. Sometimes aeroplanes were assembled on the other side of Africa, at Takoradi, and flown laboriously across the central area of the continent—a distance of 3,000 miles. Although 1,300 aircraft were sent to reinforce the Middle East between January and June 1941, a count taken in May of that year showed that only 400 modern aircraft were serviceable there.

Churchill sent a growl to Wavell that, with an army of half a million men at his disposal, he was hard put to it to find an active brigade. It was not surprising. African troops, who were unsuited to operations north of the Sahara, accounted for 132,000 of them. Moreover, convoys took three months to traverse the 12,000 miles of sea between Britain and Egypt.[3] Three months! In that space of time a convoy could cross the Atlantic four times, or make four trips to Archangel. For Rommel the sea

passage to Europe, that between Sicily and Tripoli, was
just over 300 miles. It is easy to see, then, how the
economy of effort which is at the heart of the Mahan
doctrine worked against Britain in North Africa.

The war in that theatre had grown up haphazard; it
had become the plaything of different impulses, inspira-
tions and purposes. The area was comparatively near on
the map and, in maritime reality, further away than
Australia. The glorious, inexpensive opportunity of 1940
had become the fretful obsession of 1941.

But to say that is not to dispose of the issue. North
Africa was the only region on the land surface of the
globe where British were fighting German troops. And
now the United States was a combatant and a rich new
vein of military equipment was about to open up to
Britain. The war in Africa must go on, with renewed
vigour and—who could doubt?—with better fortune.

Churchill braced himself for the debates with Roosevelt
and the American military leaders, mobilizing all his power
of advocacy, the sweep of his imagination, his formidable
grasp of the minutiae as well as the grand outlines of the
war, and his immense prestige, in order to persuade the
United States to accept the British design for victory.

The task to which he addressed himself called for some
boldness: the Americans were, presumably, aware not
only of their strength, but also of Britain's weakness. Nor
was there any conspicuous reason why they should adopt,
ready-made, a British approach to the war which, so far,
could show little success.

Lord Beaverbrook, to whom was assigned the duty of
dealing with the Americans on the question of war production, had what seemed a somewhat easier task than
that of his Prime Minister. Churchill was to convert his

host to the idea that the war was not only a joint business but was, in fact, a continuation and extension of a war which Britain had been fighting for twenty-eight months. Beaverbrook's mission was to open the eyes of the most sanguine and generous nation on earth to an awareness of its own potential power and to dazzle it with the spectacle of its own prospective bounty.

The branches of the Christmas tree would be loaded with gifts unimaginable. And Santa Claus had brought with him a large sack. Empty.


In Washington, the weather sharpened and brightened for the festal days. The city, truly a capital in its marble apparel, retreated for a while into a kind of provincial nullity. The revolutionary generals on their pedestals in Lafayette Square looked out on streets that were deserted save for a knot of worshippers hurrying to church or an occasional British visitor bent on some secular mission.

Sir Charles Wilson (later Lord Moran), the Prime Minister's physician, wearing a pair of black woollen gloves and somehow looking like a spry and busy Jesuit in an old-fashioned Protestant drawing, walked briskly from his lodging to visit his illustrious patient at the White House, pondering the while who knew what literary *coup*, still unsuspected by the public.

Scarlet poinsettias took the place of holly (for English eyes) in the decorations. At the Foundry Methodist Church, President and Prime Minister worshipped side by side. On the morning after Pearl Harbour, the minister of the church, Dr. Harris, had invited Lord Halifax to attend his Christmas Day service. He explained how his church had come to have its name. During the 1812 war between the United States and Britain, a local blacksmith who had a foundry there was also a Methodist preacher. He had

vowed to build a church on the site where a British attack
was repulsed.⁴ In this relic of an ancient war, Franklin D.
Roosevelt and Winston S. Churchill sang together "O
Little Town of Bethlehem".

> *Yet in thy dark streets shineth*
> *The everlasting Light—*
> *The hopes and fears of all the years*
> *Are met in thee tonight.*

In the dusk, the lights of the President's Christmas tree
glimmered on the lawn outside the White House.

Lord Halifax, at the British Embassy, entertained a
large company of his newly-arrived fellow-countrymen—
"Rather a scratch meal, I'm afraid"—but the Embassy
silver was out in glistening strength; the Armada screen
glowed in gold, black and scarlet, and after dinner the
Ambassador took his guests by motor coach to a cinema,
thus shortening the period of mutual embarrassment.

Far away, that day, Hong Kong surrendered to the
Japanese.

Meanwhile the more serious business of the Washington
visit went forward at speed. The hour was grave. One
after another, the strongholds were tumbling. Wake
Island had surrendered; Manila was doomed. Only the
eyes of ignorance or invincible optimism could underesti-
mate the threat to Singapore.

Churchill, who had won the hard hearts of the American newspapermen at a press conference and captivated
Congress—but not Lord Halifax ("Personally I did not
think it so very good")—by one of his greatest speeches,
gained at least a provisional acceptance of his strategic
ideas from the President's advisers.

At a dinner given by William S. Knudsen, Beaverbrook

met some of the chiefs of America's productive effort: Leon Henderson, an aggressive and talkative economist; Sydney Hillman of the Garment Workers' Union, spokesman of labour, wearing the red tie that was perhaps all that was left of a Socialist past, and speaking in a thick Bronx accent; Herbert Emmerich, short, bald, with exceptionally tiny hands, pleasant and intelligent, lifted into the Civil Service from an academic past and now permanent head of the Office of Production Management.

Knudsen had brought from his native land the stature and customs of Denmark—the bow from the waist, the *rund skaal* which opens dinner. It was said of him that, if you gave him a factory to organize, he would by some intuitive process known only to himself lay out the machinery in magic fashion. His interest seemed invariably to begin, if it did not end, with the question, "What does it weigh?" He resembled some slow-moving but immensely skilful craftsman—a watchmaker, say—rather than a head of General Motors.

Beaverbrook addressed this audience on the congenial topic of what Britain was doing and what—so much more —the United States could do. To any listener who knew the man, it was an outstanding performance, an unsurpassed exercise in the higher diplomacy. The arts of the old salesman, the propagandist, the evangelist, were deployed with the assurance of genius. The quality of the speech—which was both more and less than a speech— did not consist in any felicity of words nor in the calculated effects of the practised orator (in this art Beaverbrook never had any talent) but rather in the relentless flow of facts, the phenomenal accuracy of the speaker's memory, his uncanny awareness of the psychology of his audience. The by-play unobtrusively contributed to the effect.

Anecdotes not only entertained the audience but

helped to establish the speaker's authority. He recalled, for example, how Averell Harriman one day at Moscow had tried to persuade Stalin to take a more favourable view of Christianity. After a time, Beaverbrook thought that this missionary effort had gone on long enough. Loyal son of the manse as he was, he said to Stalin: "Promise me that if you become a Christian you'll become a Presbyterian."

At this point, Morris Wilson, a brilliant Canadian banker and an old friend of Beaverbrook's, interrupted the story: "I thought you were going to say, 'Promise me that if you *cannot* see your way to becoming a Christian, you'll become a Presbyterian.'" Morris Wilson was a Methodist.

After a time, comedy was put aside and the main theme took over, uninterrupted.

Playing a kind of sustained obligato to the solo, the rest of Mr. Knudsen's British guests may well have seemed to their host numb and tongue-tied. Among them only Hugh Weeks, the economist (now Sir Hugh Weeks, C.M.G.), put in an effective word now and then. The evening belonged to Beaverbrook. Perhaps it was the greatest of all his personal contributions during the war.

His purpose was to inflame those American industrial leaders with the scale of effort, so much vaster than they had contemplated up to that moment, which the United States was called on to make. His success was to be revealed in a day or two. In the meantime, the men round Knudsen's dinner table were at once stunned and dazzled by the vision of an urgent need and a breath-taking enterprise. Even the voluble Leon Henderson was overcome.

While the cause of Anglo-American collaboration prospered in Washington the sky darkened in Asia.

Manila fell.

Various portents suggested that it would be unwise for Churchill to delay his return to London a day longer than was necessary. It seemed that opinion at home was disturbed and likely to become more so.

Every day, Beaverbrook received from one of his political secretaries in London, David Farrer, a synopsis of opinions in the British newspapers. The summary naturally singled out matter on which the Government was being criticized, while taking for granted the general chorus of approval of Ministers in the press. However, an unaccustomed reader might not make allowance for this inherent bias. And, as it chanced, there was one reader unaccustomed and far from pleased.

Churchill, who had been shown one of the summaries by Beaverbrook, asked to have them sent to him as a regular service. Thus, unknown to the sender in London, his daily infusions of candour were circulated throughout the British Mission and read by the Prime Minister.

"Who," he asked Beaverbrook testily, "is this fellow Farrer?"

In consequence, Thomson, a member of Beaverbrook's personal staff in Washington, was given the urgent task of telephoning to London the warning that the press summaries were receiving an embarrassing measure of publicity. But how was this to be done privately when all transatlantic telephone conversations were monitored and circulated throughout the mission? The problem was made harder by the fact that Farrer had gone to the country, had not left a telephone number, and could not be found. Another member of Beaverbrook's staff in London was sought. Then a new difficulty arose. How was one to explain to a bewildered civil servant, traced to his home in Hampstead, why certain cables, which he did not know were being sent, must at all costs be amended? After attempts to convey the message by hints had failed miserably, the position was stated with terse frankness. A record of this transatlantic conversation in all its lame tergiversation and final disclosure was, next morning, circulated throughout the British Mission, where it edified those who could understand it.

Although from that moment the Prime Minister was shielded from the transmitted stings of the *News Chronicle*'s leader-writer, his own instinct told him that this was not the time to tarry on a foreign strand.

While he relaxed for a day or two at a villa on the Florida coast, news was brought him which accorded ill with the pleasant sunshine and the tepid sea. Not simply were the Japanese hurrying to their goal so rapidly that the flags on the war maps could not keep pace with them, but trouble had appeared in an unexpected form in the Mediterranean. Italian frogmen had eluded watchers in Alexandria harbour and had sunk two British battleships while they lay at anchor. For the moment, there was no British fleet in the Eastern Mediterranean.

The tidings would remain hidden from the public at home and, with luck, from the enemy. But they were a sharp reminder to the Prime Minister, if he needed anything of the sort, that war is a prolonged and changing emergency which demands unremitting vigilance. There was, too, no lack of sombre news which could not be kept from the public. While the British mission lingered in Washington, the Japanese, pressing southward in Malaya, entered Kuala Lumpur.

The darkening sky was, however, lit by a sudden flash of brilliant sunshine. On 6 January, President Roosevelt announced to Congress that, in the year 1942, 45,000 operational aircraft, 45,000 tanks, 8,000,000 tons of merchant shipping and other warlike supplies in proportion would be produced in the United States. More was promised for later on.

Figures of such magnitude called for no special insight on the part of the public to make their effect upon the imagination. They were immense; they were within the capacity of American industry; they were, in part, the outcome of the intense campaign of persuasion on which Beaverbrook had been engaged ever since he set foot in Washington. To take one example: Knudsen had proposed a programme for 1942 of 30,000 aircraft and 30,000 tanks. Both targets were raised by fifty per cent. While Knudsen had agreed that the American automobile companies could not convert more than fifteen per cent of their plants to war production, Beaverbrook had said pointedly that plant conversion in Britain had reached a hundred per cent.[5]

Beaverbrook, working in intimate harmony with Harry Hopkins, the President's closest personal representative, had brought about a revolution in the thinking of the American production chiefs. His buoyancy had proved infectious. Whether he or Hopkins should have more credit for the achievement may be a matter of dispute but it is not of importance.

Churchill, cabling the results to London, said: "Max has been magnificent and Hopkins a godsend." Something like a benevolent conspiracy between Harry Hopkins, the frail American welfare worker, and Beaverbrook, the forceful Canadian newspaper proprietor, "needling the administration with the sarcastic politeness that makes him effective",[6] seems to have sprung into life. Different in so many ways, they had in common fire, fanaticism and a partiality for short cuts.

At times during the visit, Churchill felt that his Minister of Supply acted altogether too much like an independent power and did not sufficiently remember that he was a member—and not even the chief member—of the British delegation. "Team spirit" was not an ideal that made much appeal to Beaverbrook, who had, nevertheless, a strange and attractive talent for personal loyalty. For his part, he felt that Churchill during the Washington talks encroached at times on ground that belonged to him as Minister of Supply. Roosevelt remarked to Halifax on the friction he detected between his two British visitors. "I cannot imagine how people go on living on their nerves as they do," said Halifax. "But perhaps you are the same." This Roosevelt denied.

Halifax, intelligent, conventional and cool, was endlessly puzzled and fascinated by Beaverbrook—"his order of life is unfathomable"—and torn between admiration and disapproval of Churchill. "The faults that people find in him," he decided on the day after the speech to Congress, "arise entirely from overwhelming self-centredness which makes him quite impervious to other people's feelings."[7]

After his return to London, Beaverbrook still nourished some resentment over the way he had been treated by the Prime Minister in Washington. But whatever Churchill may have felt about Beaverbrook's tendency at times to take his own way, he had no reason to complain of the ferment which he had made among the American industrialists. Roosevelt was, no doubt, himself a party to the Hopkins–Beaverbrook plot, if such a thing could be said to exist. On the eve of his speech to Congress he arbitrarily revised upwards some of the production targets. The President, like Beaverbrook, was a man temperamentally attracted by big, round figures.

The branches of the Christmas tree in Washington were burdened and bejewelled with gifts beyond the dreams of all but the most sanguine.

**A week after the publication of Roosevelt's breath-taking**

munitions programme, the British mission left Washington. The secret of the departure was well kept by the thousands of people to whom it was imparted. The train steamed out of a deserted and guarded station in a northward direction, apparently for Baltimore.

It pulled up at six o'clock next morning at Norfolk, Virginia, where three flying-boats waited on a mother-of-pearl sea under a smoky salmon-pink sky. They were to carry the party towards bluer water, greater warmth, along a course flecked by brilliant trails of orange gulfweed, towards white beaches and low nook-shotten islands: Bermuda.

From there, Churchill, Beaverbrook, two chiefs of staff and Sir Charles Wilson went on by flying-boat to England, not without hazard. This change of plan gave particular pleasure to Lord Beaverbrook, who had not relished the prospect of another tedious and comfortless Atlantic crossing.

While these important personages flew eastwards, the leader-writer of *The Times*, in his office in Printing House Square, was arranging his thoughts on the Far Eastern war for his readers: "The enemy has moved at the rate of about a hundred miles a week down the western side (of the Malay peninsula) since he crossed the Thai border. The danger to Singapore is already grave. . . . The value of Singapore is so great that there should be no thought of sacrifice involved when it comes to the decisive struggle."[8] These reflections met Churchill's eyes when he arrived in England. He had returned not a day too soon.

The rest of the British mission to Washington reconciled themselves with no difficulty at all to a return voyage by sea without the company of their fomidable leaders. The homeward voyage was accomplished in a mere seven days and it was noticeable that the standard of the films exhibited after dinner had greatly improved.

# CHAPTER IV

# *Forebodings*

*There is no greater fatuity than a political judgment
dressed in a military uniform.*
—David Lloyd George, *War Memoirs*, vol. 2, p. 751

*The world attaches wisdom to him that guesses right.*
—Nelson, *Dispatches*, vol. 6, p. 192

THE BRITAIN TO WHICH Churchill and his companions returned in mid-January 1942 was already the most thoroughly mobilized nation in the world, far more so than the Germans, for instance. Forty-nine per cent of her total occupied population worked for the state; women, like men, were subject to conscription, a servitude which none of the other belligerents dared—or needed—to impose on its subjects.[1]

Rationed, cramped, controlled, forced into camp or factory, the islanders endured the fine comb of a military socialism that was both harsh and efficient. They endured because it was necessary and because, in their hearts, they knew that it was the penalty exacted for their own laziness and folly in the past. Baldwin, Chamberlain—and one might add Cripps, Attlee—the "appeasers"—what had they been after all but so many purveyors of an article in keen public demand! It is always more pleasant—and in the short run more rewarding—to conceal evil than to do good.

The war had already run through three separate phases. The first, which ended in defeat and humiliation at Dunkirk, had, for the British, one compensation. They had always claimed to be an island. Now they found that they were one. "We stand alone." It was, in a way, a relief to a people which had become a great power while keeping the mentality of a small one, which had never been quite at its ease as an empire and which had as its national vice, not megalomania, but self-sufficiency. The British, who cared little about democracy (a conception too abstract for their liking), less about Europe (a foreign continent), and not a great deal about the Empire (too grandiose), did care passionately about Britain. Every Englishman, is at heart, a little Englander. He is unconsciously arrogant; he is pursued by cosiness. There was no cosiness about the British in 1940.

Stripped of that veneer of casualness, almost of flippancy, in which they like to disguise their real nature, they became the men their ancestors had been, serious, hard and beset. And Churchill spoke to them as nobody had spoken to them since Elizabeth talked to her troops at Tilbury three centuries and a half before. Giving his words to their thoughts, he won a lasting tenancy in their hearts.

The second phase ended more auspiciously: the decisive repulse of the *Luftwaffe* in the Battle of Britain was followed by the ordeal of the Blitz. "These poor people," said General Sir Hastings Ismay (later Lord Ismay) as he looked out on a London bus queue one brilliant summer evening in 1940. "They don't know what is coming to them!" On the first evening of the Blitz, an eminent industrialist, Sir Charles Craven, remarked: "Now we shall see if the British people have guts."

It is not, it never has been, "guts" that the British lack. Their shortcomings are otherwise. And, the Blitz over, one of those failings proved to be a virtue. Only a few of them, untypical souls, asked how the war was to be won. And this was just as well. It was not a time for intellectual curiosity.

Had they read the long discourse in which Mr. Churchill set out his recipe for victory to President Roosevelt in the autumn of 1940, they would not have been impressed. Had they put the question to the Prime Minister direct, he would have answered as he did more than once in private conversation. "If we hold on, sooner or later Hitler will make a mistake."

Even if there was no evidence to support it (but there probably was) the answer was perceptive and, as far as it could be, satisfying. On 22 June, 1941, Hitler made his mistake: his invasion of Russia opened the third phase of the war.

The British people were, simultaneously, relieved and demoted. They had acquired what every naval power longs for when at war: an ally on land capable of engaging the mass of the enemy's army. But their own military effort soon came to look puny. They had lost their monopoly of sacrifice and heroism. And, having put up with one disappointment after another, they now began to question the efficacy of their leadership.

The war in the desert, after a glorious first act, had become a fatiguing drama in which the hopes of the audience were raised too high and frustrated too often. Even the flourishes of Churchill ("The Desert Army may add a page to history which will rank with Blenheim and Waterloo. The eyes of all nations are upon you") began to pall a little when the sequel was only a fresh demonstration that German leadership was more professional and German weapons more efficient.

But the grumbles of the public could end only in perplexity; for in the conditions of total war the normal processes of democracy are severely inhibited. The people cannot inform themselves because the newspapers are subjected to a sharp and necessary censorship. Parliament cannot carry out effectively its tasks of probing, discussing, judging and correcting. It cannot insist on questions being answered because it does not know which questions ought to be asked. Besides, criticism must be muted lest the enemy be too much encouraged.

As 1941 drew to a close, there was a further limitation on controversy: the Prime Minister was the all-highest war lord, rejoicing in his responsibility. He stood firm against any significant change in the system by which Britain waged war. And he was, in the eyes of almost all, the indispensable leader of the nation.

Then, on a nation already troubled and confused, fell the thunderbolt of the Japanese onslaught. Already there had been grumblings in the House of Commons and the newspapers about the exasperating lack of success in the Western Desert. And now, suddenly, the huge tragedy of the Far East had loomed up: two battleships lost and Hong Kong about to fall; Malaya invaded and Singapore in danger. The House had been ominously quiet when, two days before leaving London on his expedition to Washington, Churchill had given it the sad news of the battleships.

The storm had blown up out of the tropical seas, and it seemed, had taken him by surprise. By surprise?

But it had been plain from the moment a trade embargo had been imposed on Japan in July 1941, five months before, cutting her off from all sources of oil, that she must lunge out with all her naval and military strength or submit to America's political demands in China. Japan's oil reserves shrank by a little each month; and the moment could be exactly foreseen after which major operations— any major operations—would become impossible for her.[2]

In these circumstances, was it likely that the Japanese soldiers and sailors would capitulate without defeat? Were they men of that kind? It would have been the wildest optimism to think so. Was it even likely that Japan, while striking at the United States, might leave Britain unassailed? Nothing of the sort was possible.

On 10 November, 1941, the Prime Minister had told his fellow-guests at the Guildhall banquet: "Should the United States become involved in war with Japan it is my duty to say that the British declaration will follow within the hour." These were martial words. They called for far-reaching changes in Britain's dispositions to meet a crisis—a "crunch"—which could not be far off.

Yet between the end of July 1941 and Japan's outbreak, Britain's air force in Malaya, roughly half what was judged to be necessary, was not reinforced. Her land forces in the peninsula received the addition of only one reconnaisance regiment, one anti-tank regiment and three field artillery regiments—although it must be said at once that disaster in Malaya was not brought about by any shortage of troops on the ground. To the Royal Navy in the area were added two capital ships, the *Prince of Wales* and the *Repulse*, which by themselves could not possibly be an effective fighting force.

It was apparently thought, however—on a mistaken analogy with the role played by the German battleship *Tirpitz* in relation to the Atlantic—that the two ships would, somehow, act as a vague threat to Japanese sea communications. In fact, the vessels could not be put to any intelligent use; they could only have been saved by immediate flight from Malayan waters; they stayed, and were destroyed.

There had been, as it seemed, a failure to give serious study and effective reinforcement to the Far East at a time when Britain was sending tanks and fighters every month to Russia and when there was a steady flow of reinforcements to Egypt. This failure was in part the outcome of a deliberate choice of priorities by the Prime Minister. As Dr. Evatt, the Australian Minister of External Affairs, complained, "By his Guildhall speech, Churchill made war with Japan inevitable. Then he did nothing to prepare for it!" Other voices had proposed a different course of action.

In May 1941, Sir John Dill, Chief of the Imperial General Staff, had written to the Prime Minister:[3] "The loss of Egypt would be a calamity . . . but it would not end the war. . . . It has been an accepted principle in our strategy that in the last resort the security of Singapore comes before that of Egypt." He went on to argue that the defences of Singapore, far below standard, should be strengthened before it was too late, by accepting losses in less vital areas.

Churchill rejected the advice, sharply: "I gather you would be prepared to face the loss of Egypt . . . rather than lose Singapore. I do not take that view."[4]

Here, then, was a head-on collision on a capital question of strategy between Churchill and his chief military adviser. Not everyone would have agreed with the Prime Minister on the issue: nor was it certain that the antithesis, as Dill and Churchill stated it, exhausted the possibilities inherent in the situation. For example, Egypt might well be kept and Rommel held at bay while permitting some diversion of forces to the Far East.

But if the choice, in the desperate summer of 1941, was indeed as the Prime Minister described it, who can say that his verdict was wrong? The menace from Japan was potential, even if it was no more than probable, but the crisis in the Middle East was real and immediate. And, for all its tremendous importance, Singapore lay on the periphery of Britain's area of concern.

Its purpose was to screen the route to Australia and New Zealand and to guard the approaches to the Indian Ocean.

But if Japan were to attack, the United States would probably be at war, and Australia and New Zealand would look eastwards and not westwards for support. If, as the result of a catastrophic chain of events, Britain found herself simultaneously at war with the three powers of the Axis, bitter necessity would compel her to shorten her front and discard some at least of the outlying fragments of the Empire.

Impressive arguments could be invoked in favour of the primacy of the Middle East over Singapore. The Nile delta and the area in its vicinity was one of the key *places d'armes* of the world. It bridged two continents. From it, forces could strike north, south, east and west. And it covered Britain's strategic source of oil in the Persian Gulf.

Would it not have been possible, however, to stand on the defensive in the Middle East and thus to spare tanks and aircraft to reinforce Malaya? That this should be done had been the opinion of the Middle East High Command after the oil sanction was imposed on Japan. But in the sharp practicality of the war, the problem was not so simple. Churchill did not enjoy full freedom of thought or action.

First of all, there was the war in Russia and the psychological and political reverberations in Britain. German armies were disposed on a vast shallow arc from Leningrad, which was pitilessly beset and savagely defended, to the Crimea, where Sebastopol held out against them. In the centre, Moscow had, by the narrowest of margins, been denied to Hitler.

Roughly speaking, the Germans had conquered nearly half of European Russia in five months of war. They had

failed to reach the main prizes which they sought:
Moscow, oil, the Donetz basin. Above all they had not
brought about the collapse of the Russian political system. But what a staggering achievement theirs had been
all the same! And who was to say what they would
accomplish when campaigning weather returned with the
spring of 1942?

The British public had watched the unfolding of the
Russian war in horror and stupefaction. More convincingly even than in the Battle of France, here was a
demonstration of the amplitude of German military
power! Battles on such a scale, defeats so vast, losses so
enormous! Yet—most astonishing of all—Russia was
still in the fight. No sign of a crack in morale, no whisper
of political discontent or disunity. A people that had
endured and survived so much might do even more to
astound the world.

So the British people waited on events with misgivings
with which a certain tincture of self-accusation was
mixed. It was not that they felt under any undue sense of
obligation to Russia. She had come into the war when
she was forced to do so, and not a minute before. Britain
in one sense owed her nothing.

True, Communist agitators—the real boneless wonders
of modern politics—tried to whip up the public to a sense
of guilt. But the zealots of the party line, loudly demanding "a Second Front now" in the West End of London,
wore, all too recognizably, the same faces as those earlier
champions of the workers who, in the summer of 1940,
demanded "deep shelters now". The old clamour was no
doubt intended to embarrass the British war effort; the
new was meant to stimulate it—in a particular direction.
It needed no excessive cynicism to see through and
discredit either of them.

However, it was necessary to consider the matter on a

different and more urgent level than that of morality. The
Russians were fighting; by the summer of 1942 they might
not be fighting. It was the merest common sense to take as
many German divisions as possible off Russia's back
while she was still in the fight. Looked at in this way, the
British military effort was hardly gratifying to reason or
national pride. To be brief, the British army was engaging
in battle two (later three) German divisions. It was doing
so with only qualified success.

The battle which had been fought in North Africa the
month before Japan came into the war ended in a retreat
by the German commander Rommel, who had lost a
third of his tanks. But British losses were heavier still,
as British armour had initially been more numerous.
Worse still, the British fleet in the Eastern Mediterranean
had been effectively destroyed. German U-boats and aircraft had regained mastery in the sea between Africa and
Sicily.

It was, of course, absurd to measure the strain on
Britain by her exertions on land against one antagonist.
Thirty German divisions remained in Western Europe
and twenty-four in reserve because a (much smaller)
British army was in being across the Channel. The Italian
Army, heavily engaged against the British, could not be
dismissed as an entirely negligible factor. There was a
British air offensive.

Above all, the quiet, deadly, unending war at sea
against U-boats, questing aircraft and surface raiders,
absorbed navy, merchant fleet and a considerable industrial effort of replacement and repair.

All this did not seem enough to one cold-eyed arith-
metician in the Kremlin who translated Britain's military
strength of, say, three million men under arms into
Russian terms. Stalin found that Britain, with the equivalent of a hundred Russian divisions in men mobilized, was

playing an unduly modest role in the war. It was easy enough to answer him, but it was not at all easy to overlook the fact that Russia seemed to be near the end of her tether.

Ivan Maisky, the Soviet Ambassador in London, warned Anthony Eden at the end of August 1941 that the Russian Government thought Britain had done little to help her ally. Maisky's grumbles to Eden were echoed all over Britain. "Feeling here has risen very high," wrote Churchill to his general in Egypt, Sir Claude Auchinleck, in October, "against what is thought to be our supine incapacity for action. I am, however, fully in control of public opinion."

This was still true two months later, when the desert battle had ended inconclusively and the typhoon from Japan was sweeping over the Empire in Eastern Asia. But the horse that Churchill rode was growing restive.

Had the war in the Middle East come to bulk too large in British strategy? Was it eating too much of the country's military resources? If this were indeed so, the explanation was that, for a long time, thinking about the Middle East had been tinctured with emotion. For a proper understanding of how this had come about, it is necessary to go back in time a year or more.

The war in the desert had prospered gloriously for Britain in 1940 at a time when utter catastrophe had overtaken her fortunes in Europe. In a chain of dazzling battles, General Richard O'Connor had all but destroyed the Italian armies (130,000 prisoners, 400 tanks, 1,290 guns) at a cost of 422 men killed. His tactics were as unconventional as they were successful. On a large scale O'Connor repeated his pre-war triumph in Palestine. Then, as Governor of Jerusalem, he had been faced with the problem of recapturing the Old City held by Arab insurgents. To take that labyrinth of alleys promised to be a

costly operation. O'Connor solved the problem by sending the Coldstream Guards to fight not on the ground but
from roof to roof. The City was captured with the loss of
one man.

In his campaign in the desert, O'Connor stood poised
by February 1941 at El Agheila, with only the remnants of
five broken Italian divisions between him and Tripoli.

"If Wavell [the Commander-in-Chief, Middle East] had
now continued his advance into Tripolitania, no resistance worthy of the name could have been mounted
against him."[5] This was the judgment of the German
General Erwin Rommel, who arrived in Tripoli on 12
February, ahead of his troops. If the British Army had
swept forward to Tripoli, this would have called for an all-
out effort in support by the Navy comparable in scale
with the operation which it mounted a little later to rescue
what it could from the defeat in Greece and Crete. In
these circumstances, the debris of the Italian Army—if
any could be said to exist—would have been rounded up
or chased over the border into Tunisia where the French
were waiting with orders to disarm and intern them. For
Tunisia formed part of the responsibility of General
Maxime Weygand, Delegate-General in French Africa
and Commander-in-Chief of French land, air and naval
forces in the region; and, faced by the prospect of an irrup-
tion into Tunisia by the Italian troops retreating before
General O'Connor, Weygand, as he later described his intentions, "considered that it would be our duty to disarm
and intern those who tried to find refuge there. I instructed General Audet [the French Commander in Tunisia] as
to the measures to be adopted in that event in disarming
the Italians and directing them to concentration camps."[6]

When the question is asked, would not Rommel have
altered his plan in these circumstances and sent his troops
not to Tripoli but to Tunis or Bizerta, these facts must be

borne in mind: the operation would have meant a breach
of the terms of the French armistice; in place of a peaceful
landing at Tripoli, there would have been a landing for
which Rommel would have had to rely on the support—
or at least the presence—of the Italian fleet; but the French
fleet in the Western Mediterranean, with two battleships,
two battle cruisers and an aircraft-carrier, was stronger
than the Italian, with one battleship at Spezia and another
at Naples.

Once ashore at Tunis, Rommel would still have been
divided by 400 miles of difficult country from the British
outposts. He would have had dubious neighbours, at best,
on his right flank. And he would not have accomplished
his object, which was to save the Italians from final destruction.

If, then, O'Connor had been allowed to continue his
westward march, there would have been no Italians left in
Africa—and if any German troops had appeared there,
they could not have rescued, although they might have replaced, the lost legions of the Duce. In so far as anything
in war can ever be, that is a certainty.

But, as it chanced, Rommel had no need to take a tragic
view of his strategic prospects in Africa.

On the very day he arrived in Tripoli (12 February,
1941), and made his sombre assessment of the situation,
Churchill was composing a telegram to General Wavell:
"Our major effort must now be to aid Greece and/or
Turkey. This rules out any serious effort against Tripoli."

Thus was announced the most disastrous British blunder of the war—disastrous tactically, disastrous strategi-
cally, and a cruel blow to the morale of the soldiers in the
desert. For them, "never glad confident morning again".
When victory came at last, it came grimly and expensively,
shorn of the headlong dash and coruscating invention of
those early battles.

The brilliant general who had designed and executed the galaxy of victories over the Italian armies was now— in those early days of 1941—in a position to seize the final spoils. But he was not allowed to snatch them. Indeed, it does not seem to have occurred to O'Connor to urge the advantages that there would be in taking Tripoli. In destroying the Italian 10th Army he had accomplished his task.

If only Wavell had been able, like Nelson, to put a telescope to his blind eye! If only he had disobeyed Churchill, as Churchill would have disobeyed! Alas, Wavell, like Sir John Dill, fell a victim to the allurements of the Greek adventure.

"In defeat, defiance." A magnificent battle-cry. But defiance, like patriotism, is not enough. Caution must be added, and cunning too. There was no caution about sending five divisions to Greece to do a job that needed— in the opinion of the War Office—twenty. And where was the cunning?

The blunder of the Greek campaign was made for honourable and even noble reasons, as blunders sometimes are. Greece—it meant Thucydides and Byron, Marathon and Thermopylae—how could it fail to appeal to Churchill's imagination, resonant with the echoes of history and literature? Greece fighting superbly against the Italians in Albania, awakening thoughts of ancient glory —how could it fail to excite the chivalry of that great and generous man?

In the argument which prevailed in the British War Cabinet and which is resumed in the message to Wavell, the gaps in the reasoning are filled in with lavish, if unobtrusive, slabs of emotion. Reason was present too, of course. It was good that Greece, after resisting Italy, should not be crushed by Germany; good that Britain, after her military failure in France, should show herself eager and able to help an ally in the Balkans.

There was also the possibility that, if she failed to do so, the Greek Government might become an active collaborator with the Germans. This was a prospect of which the British Cabinet heard a great deal during the critical days when the decision was being taken.

On the other hand, it was fanciful to suppose that, if Britain could sustain Greece, Turkey might then come into the war at Britain's side. Nevertheless, this hope seems to have been cherished. Turkey was the subject of a recurring delusion that haunted Churchill throughout the war.

The great mass of argument—or so it seems to the student made wise by events—was arrayed against the operation: the manifest error of diverting thought and effort from a prosperous campaign on the very eve of its final victory; the risks attendant on leaving any Italian forces, however feeble, in Africa, where they would certainly be reinforced; the advantages of setting up a base in Tripoli, and of renewing contact with the French in Tunisia.

These weighty considerations, and the brilliant hopes they opened up, did not prevail with the ministers in London.

At the last minute, Churchill turned cool towards the expedition—almost at the same time as Wavell succumbed to its appeal. Why the Commander-in-Chief in Cairo made this unfortunate *volte-face* is unknown. Perhaps he, a passionately literate soldier, fell victim like his Prime Minister to the witchery of Hellas. At any rate, he convinced himself that he could both save Greece and continue the campaign in the desert. Lord Beaverbrook, Minister of Aircraft Production, member of the War Cabinet, opposed the Greek enterprise vigorously but to no effect.

In the upshot, Greece could not be saved. Crete was overrun. Thirty thousand men were lost, the equipment of four and a half divisions; three cruisers and six destroyers

The magnificent New Zealand division was sacrificed. "Never, never again," protested the New Zealand Prime Minister, Fraser, "must New Zealanders be allowed to fight without air cover." And Rommel's Afrika Korps was given the opportunity to establish itself in Tripolitania.

This was the price paid for allowing strategy to be dictated by high politics and fine feelings. It was not, however, the full price.

By unlocking the door of Africa to Rommel, the British had made it harder for themselves to reinforce the Far East on the scale which very soon it manifestly needed. The ships lost off Crete, the tanks and aircraft (850 of the first and 1,300 of the second) poured into the Middle East after the first German victories in the desert, might have been used to strengthen Singapore even if they could not have saved it.

But Britain's military strength in the Middle East grew by what it fed on, defeat. Annoyance at his own error in admitting Rommel to Africa simmered in Churchill's mind into a pugnacious resolve to be avenged on the intruder. In him, the duellist was never far beneath the surface of the statesman, and in Rommel—"may I say, across the havoc of war, a great general"—Churchill thought he discerned an antagonist worthy of his blade. It was his misfortune that he became emotionally involved with one who was, for all his brilliance, a minor figure among the ranks of his adversaries.

As the months of 1941 rolled by, another factor came to affect the disposition of British forces—the Russian resistance, the Second Front agitation, the need to placate what was sound and honest in the demand that more be done to take the weight of battle off the reluctant ally.

Only in the Middle East, as it seemed, were circumstances favourable for a response that would go beyond an empty gesture of assistance. The clamour to do something drowned the debate about what it was best to do. And the protagonists of the Second Front, contemptuous of the Desert War, ironically abetted Churchill, who detested them, in his determination to fight it.

As an inevitable result of this concentration on the Middle East, the Far East, where there was still no war, was kept on short commons of supplies and attention. Britain, which in the first seven months of 1941 reinforced the Middle East with 200,000 men and a wealth of armour and aircraft, and in August 1941 offered the Turks four divisions and twenty R.A.F. squadrons, had still only three divisions, and 180 aircraft, to defend Malaya. There was no armour.

On the eve of the Japanese attack, there were 128 R.A.F. squadrons in Britain, thirty-five in the Middle East and twelve in the Far East. There were thirty-six divisions in Britain, thirteen, building up to twenty-five, in the Middle East and (as has been said) three in Malaya. This distribution of strength can hardly be regarded as satisfactory. It would be explained if Churchill had, in his heart, written off Malaya as indefensible. But this was not so.

Was his absorption, mental and emotional, in the Middle East so complete that he could bring himself neither to spare the resources for Malaya nor even to devote a close enough scrutiny to its military problems to reveal them as they were, in reality and not in rhetoric? For example, "the fortress of Singapore", of which he loved to speak, was only half a fortress, as an hour's study or ten minutes' interrogation of experts would have informed him.[7]

It may be admitted that adequate and timely reinforcement of Malaya meant something more than a diversion of strength from other quarters. Above all, it required that the troops already in Malaya should be given intensive special training. It involved the postponement of cherished projects in the desert (which, as it turned out, were frustrated) or in Turkey (which came to nothing anyway).

In the month of January 1942, Britain lurched towards the greatest military disaster in her history, the consequences of which would be almost as far-reaching as those of the surrender at Yorktown, unprepared in plans or resources for what was in store. Some of those whose forebodings drew for them the image of what lay ahead took comfort in the thought that no more could have been done. They were wrong.

# CHAPTER V

# *Advance from Moscow*

*God does not want to do everything Himself.*
—Machiavelli, *The Prince*, chapter 26

THE DAY AFTER the Prime Minister's return to London, the newspapers announced that another of the chief actors had appeared—or re-appeared—on the British political stage. Sir Stafford Cripps, who, since the first days of the Churchill administration, had been British Ambassador in Moscow, returned from his embassy without an excessive welcome from the British Government.

Cripps was a well-to-do barrister and an independent-minded Socialist member of Parliament who was at odds with the leadership of the Labour Party. In fact, on his return to England he was ostracized by Labour Ministers and under-secretaries. He had a notable power of lucid and compelling speech and a character which seemed to reproach, in its crystalline integrity, the dusty compromises of public life.

Politics being, in large measure, a cynical comedy acted by zanies, Cripps seemed ill-suited for the cast: too intelligent to be a dupe; too honest to be a confidence-man. He was a conspicuously devout Anglican. And, although he was without the cruder forms of popular appeal, there could be no doubt that he gave off a kind of frosty magnetism.

Might not a man of his type, stiff, dedicated, ascetic,

have a message for the public in so grim an emergency? The country had been led by a Cavalier. Might not the hour have struck for a Roundhead? With no marked enthusiasm, the men at the head of Britain's affairs conceded that indeed it might.

Vaguely discontented with the modest scale and comparative failure of the military effort, the setback in the desert, the impending *débâcle* in Malaya, the public felt that some steel had gone out of the nation's backbone. Was there not a flagging in moral fibre and spiritual purpose?

Dr. William Temple, then Archbishop of York and in a few weeks to become Archbishop of Canterbury, was at the head of those who put difficult questions like that. A few days after the return of Cripps from Russia, Temple asked Convocation at York what the country was fighting for, what were its war aims? Retribution for the monstrous crimes that Hitler and his associates had committed? This has been numbered by the Prime Minister among our purposes. But we must take care. "For it is easy to slide from the obligation to impose retribution into the desire to exact vengenace: and this is naked evil." He told a luncheon club in Manchester that the war was essentially a spiritual struggle, between two sharply contrasted conceptions of the principles on which human life should be founded: "In the name of what are we resisting the Nazis?"

The question was characteristic of the mood through which the nation was passing: discontented with its achievements, conscious of the need for a fresh impetus, it began to ask—after twenty-eight months of war—what it was fighting for, and it awaited a new trumpet to sound the call to a war which would also be a crusade.

The Archbishop was not the only man to ask the question and his answer was not the only one to be supplied. A section of the public was dissatisfied with the Prime

Minister's refusal to import a social, reforming element into his thinking. "If democracy is to conquer it must convince its own people and others too, that it is on the march, that it has not finished what it has to say to mankind. . . . But reconstruction has been put in the hands of a minister who would not be entrusted with anything really important."[1]

A serving officer who was also a Labour candidate reported[2] a silent revolution in opinion, dividing the country on lines different from the old party lines. A corporate sense was growing up among those in uniform, most of whom had never voted. After all, it was six years since there had been a general election. "There seems a great opening for a new party. It must advocate a 'classless' society and aim at evoking a patriotism of the kind which Russia has managed to inspire."

From the Left, then, as well as from the leaders of the Church, came evidence of a spiritual hunger, of the call for a new shepherd for the sheep.

Who, at that moment, seemed more providentially arrived to fill the role than Cripps? It was of little importance that he was said to lack humour ("Stafford saw a joke last week—by appointment") and, an even worse defect in a statesman, judgment. He came from Moscow, at fifty-one, a man in his prime, serious, intense, trailing behind him the crimson clouds of Russia's ordeal and sacrifice.

The return of the paladin came as no surprise to the most casual student of the Left-wing press. On January 3, the Liberal *News Chronicle* announced that Cripps would soon return and might enter the Cabinet. Three days later, the *Manchester Guardian* said, more guardedly, that he would not throw in his lot with any "embryonic" opposition to the Government. But if any member of the Government hopefully supposed that the Ambassador might be expected to return meekly to his post, a leading article in *The Times* would enlighten him. The choice before Cripps was, as it appeared to the newspaper, between a seat in the War Cabinet and a seat on the front opposition bench. "His course will be dictated by a high sense of duty."

That it had also been influenced by an astute sense of timing could hardly be doubted. There could be no question that the newspapers thought the proper place for Sir Stafford was in high office and that he embodied, better than any other public man, a certain severe and intense attitude to the war situation. The *Daily Mirror*, noting that Cripps had given bathrooms to his tenants, predicted that he would soon take his proper place among the men who directed the fortunes of the nation.

Nevertheless, Cripps was, in some respects, an odd choice as an inspiring leader in the nation's fight for life. In the years of "appeasement" he had written in the Socialist weekly *Forward*, "Every possible effort should be made to stop recruiting for the armed forces."[3] In writing this, Cripps was in conformity with the main body of Left-wing thinking in those far-off, peacetime days when British politics, on one side and the other, seemed to be dominated, not by men, but by superannuated children. "The country, in fact, was faced with an astonishing paradox. The Conservatives were in favour of armaments on the understanding that they would not be used, and the Labour Opposition was in favour of using armaments on the understanding that they were not to be provided."[4]

A great deal had happened in the six years which had rolled by since Cripps's *Forward* article. Much had been learned and much changed. Many had repented and some had been saved. Saved? Promoted to the highest places in a country at war!

Among them were men who were antagonistic to Cripps's social ideals and men who shared the ideals but had driven him out of their party. In January 1939, a few months before the outbreak of war, Cripps, then a member of the national executive of the Labour Party, was expelled for what were called "Popular Front Activities".

In those days, the Spanish Civil War was approaching its final phase. Barcelona was about to fall to Franco, a general who enjoyed Fascist and Nazi support. This prospect brought despondency to all who believed that they were witnessing the unfolding of a vast ideological conflict, of which the war in Spain was only an early chapter.

Cripps had sent a circular to local Labour Party branches demanding an emergency party conference to consider the international situation and the possibility of an alliance with other bodies to defeat the Chamberlain Government. The proposal raised the spectre, horrific to conventional Labour eyes, of an association with Communists. When called on to withdraw the circular and reaffirm his allegiance to the party, Sir Stafford had defended himself with vigour. After wrestling in vain with the conscience of the heretic for an hour and a half, the Labour Party Executive (with one dissenting voice) drove him forth. "Silent and morose," Sir Stafford left the party offices at Transport House. He was not silent for long.

At the Queen's Hall in London that night he told an "Arms for Spain" rally that he was still convinced that the working-class movement must be the core and centre of every anti-Fascist drive. "I must still continue, however, to tell the people the direction in which alone I am convinced their salvation can lie." After hearing these rousing words, a demonstration 3,000 strong marched down Whitehall, chanting, as it passed Downing Street, "We demand arms for Spain".

Thus, at the moment he returned from Moscow, Cripps was a Member of Parliament (for his constituency at East Bristol remained faithful to him) but a member of no political party. In the circumstances, this was not a handi-cap.

Very soon the role he meant to play became clearer. He would become the embodiment of a more strenuous and unsparing war to match the grandeurs and miseries of Russia. He would speak with the authority of one who had come from that fabulous land, and it mattered not to the effectiveness of his utterances that his embassy had been a bitterly frustrating experience.

During eight weeks he had seen neither Stalin nor Molotov. When the Germans came too near to Moscow he had been bundled off with other diplomats to Kuiby-shev, five hundred miles to the east. Not long before this happened, there had been a humiliation of a different kind.

Lord Beaverbrook arrived in Moscow with Averell Harriman on a brief and busy mission concerned with military supplies. It was an hour of intense military crisis in Russia—28 September, 1941, just two days before the Germans launched their offensive against Moscow to the south of Bryansk. "The last great decisive battle of this year," as Hitler called it, was about to open.

Beaverbrook, who had been almost from the beginning the vehement champion of every kind of encouragement for the Russians, was immediately congenial to Stalin. He, for his part, summed up the Georgian as a man of cour-age with a ruthless talent for organization, who would stay in the fight to the bitter end. He was not one easily impressed in such matters, but, ever afterwards, he spoke in deep admiration of Stalin's "intellectual brilliance". This quality had been shown in an extraordinary grasp of the most complex problems of munitions and strategy.

Beaverbrook had the good sense not to ask his host searching questions about the progress of the war which he knew would either be evaded or resented. Rather, he brought to the encounter all the gifts of the practised journalist, the sense of "news", the alertness of observation. Before leaving Britain, for example, he had taken pains to get in touch by letter with Rudolf Hess, knowing how interested—and suspicious—the Russians were about this uninvited guest of Britain's. He was able to take with him to Moscow some interesting tit-bits of news. Hess, he told Stalin, seemed to have reached an advanced state of paranoia. He believed that attempts were being made to drug him. Once he had tried to commit suicide by throwing himself over a stair headpost and in doing so had broken his thigh on a banister.

Seated next to Stalin at the customary Kremlin banquet, Beaverbrook noticed that the Russian leader ate his caviar with a knife. He was served with different food from the others and, while the rest of the company had wine poured into their glasses, Stalin had a bottle of his own, over which he kept a glass inverted. Many and ingenious were the devices employed by Beaverbrook in the course of the banquet to taste the wine in Stalin's bottle. He did not succeed. He observed, too, that Stalin spoke of Leningrad as Petersburg.

At the start of the talks Stalin offered Oumansky, Soviet Ambassador in Washington and an old acquaintance of Beaverbrook's, as the interpreter, along with a British interpreter of Beaverbrook's choice. Beaverbrook replied that he would be content with one interpreter alone—not Oumansky, however, but Litvinov, former Soviet ambassador in London (and later Soviet Foreign Minister), who was married to an Englishwoman.

This being acceptable, Litvinov, who at the time was living in retirement, was disinterred from his lodging and brought to the Kremlin, miserably dressed in a shabby suit and broken shoes. Stalin noticed that Beaverbrook had taken in these details. At the next session, Litvinov appeared considerably smartened up. He performed his duties as interpreter with great competence. But there was always a door open with a dark room beyond it where another listener sat to serve as a check on Litvinov.

It was Oumansky, however, who during the stay in Moscow unveiled for Beaverbrook the grim picture of the battle that was raging. While they were walking together across Red Square, that bleak urban steppe under the walls of the Kremlin, Oumansky said that the Russian southern front had been destroyed. The situation was catastrophic. It was indeed. On 2 October, while Beaverbrook, Harriman and their advisers were still negotiating in Moscow, Guderian's panzers had advanced 150 miles from their starting point and captured Orel at a time when the trams were still running in the town. It was no time to dally.

Talks were speeded up. The obligatory festive farewells took place in an atmosphere of tension. On the last night a private performance of *Swan Lake* was arranged for the foreign guests by the Chief of Security. Beaverbrook noticed that Litvinov was not present. He asked the Russian public prosecutor if he could have some words of conversation with Litvinov. It was made clear to him that, for Litvinov's sake, this would be unwise.

It was natural enough, then, if in the bustle and lurking anxieties of the moment, Cripps was left out of the talks so that he scarcely knew what had been decided. After all, on 4 October, when the Anglo-American mission was still in the Russian capital, "the great panic" was only twelve days ahead, when thousands fled from the city, which was proclaimed in a state of siege. But Cripps felt that he, the King's representative, had been treated with something less than due courtesy by Beaverbrook, a man to whom he was temperamentally antipathetic.

Cripps was, in fact, the subject, or victim, of one of

Beaverbrook's favourite anecdotes. When he had visited Mussolini in 1936 he found the Duce deeply interested in British politics and convinced that the Socialists were coming to power. "Who," he asked Beaverbrook, "is the coming man in British Socialism?" At that time Clement Attlee was a comparatively obscure figure. "Cripps," said Beaverbrook, although at that time Cripps had been driven into exile by the party.

"Does he have any money?" asked Mussolini.

"Yes," said Beaverbrook, "he got it through his wife."

"What does she get her money from?"

"Eno's Fruit Salts," said Beaverbrook, explaining the purpose of the preparation.

Mussolini roared with laughter. "We use castor oil in Italy," he said.

Beaverbrook's humour had a foundation in truth, although it underrated the extent to which Cripps's earnings at the Bar contributed to his fortune. By 1939, his Bar practice was believed to be bringing in between £30,000 and £35,000 a year. Lady Cripps was a granddaughter of James Crossley Eno, a manufacturer of a proprietary medicine, who died worth £1,611,607.

On Beaverbrook's return to England from Moscow he conveyed his impression that Cripps counted for little in Russia: some echo of this disparaging report may have been wafted to the exile in the steppes and speeded his footsteps homewards.

There were, in fact, good reasons for Cripps's failure in Russia. A man of his type, a stiff-necked English Socialist, was no more likely to appeal to Stalin than he did to Beaverbrook. Another matter may also have weighed against him. In April 1941, Cripps had delayed during sixteen days before passing on to Stalin Churchill's "sure information from a trusted agent" about Hitler's warlike designs on Russia. Churchill's hope was that, warned in time, Stalin might co-operate with Britain in the Balkans, thus causing the Germans to postpone their Russian enterprise.

"Mr. Churchill's design was unhappily frustrated by the egotism of the Ambassador. Sir Stafford Cripps, who had recently addressed a long letter to M. Vishinsky, to which he attached great importance, was unwilling to spoil its effect by delivering the Prime Minister's message to Stalin . . . The incident was inexcusable."[5]

Whether this exhibition of vanity had any effect on Cripps's popularity with the Russian leader cannot, of course, be proved. He suffered from another handicap for which he could not be blamed. His presence in Russia was a constant reminder to his hosts of the months in which they had been Hitler's dupes and Cripps had, on his own behalf or that of his Government, belatedly or in time, sounded the note of foreboding.

Putting behind him any discouraging recollection of his sojourn in Russia, Sir Stafford on his return to England became with no delay the champion of help for Russia and the exponent of a sacrificial war on the Russian model. Kuibyshev forgotten, the heroic lights of Maloyaroslavetz and Sebastopol gleamed through his pale spectacles.

In his stern attitude he did not lack support. Others read the same message in the sky over Moscow and Malaya. In the *Sunday Pictorial*, Hugh Cudlipp wrote: "Britain will begin to stand up to Germany when the civilians are mobilized and disciplined just as strictly as the men and women in fighting service. Good-bye to freedom and privilege: it would mean all that."[6] Thus already the soil was being prepared for the seed Cripps would sow and harvest, although even he might not be ready to go so far as the newspaper: "There is only one way to end profiteering, the filthiest crime of the war. First offence, flog them. Second offence, shoot them."[7]

He spoke in moving terms to a press conference in London of the enormous cost in terms of human suffering, and domestic tragedy, of the Russian war, fought as it was in sub-zero cold. He conveyed the broad hint that many young Russian officers had been promoted to high commands, "a lesson a lot of countries might learn". The significance of a remark like this did not escape attention in government circles in London. The *Daily Mirror* proclaimed: "Cripps is to take his proper place among the men who direct the fortunes of the nation. He may, at last, become a member of the Cabinet." While that event seemed every day more likely, Cripps sent a message to *Izvestia* which epitomized what he had come to represent: "Let us shorten the world's agony," he said, "by the intensity of our efforts."

## CHAPTER VI

# *"Our duty to overthrow him"*

*Each victory doth help us some other to win.*
*—Church Hymnary*, Hymn 561

*Our time cannot be more usefully employed during a*
*war than in examining how it has been conducted, and*
*settling the degree of confidence that may be reposed in*
*those, to whose care are entrusted our reputations, our*
*fortunes, our lives.*
—William Pitt the elder, 1740

ON 21 JANUARY, 1942, the Prime Minister took a
whisky and soda after a meeting of the Defence Committee* with Eden, Lord Beaverbrook and A. V. Alexander,
First Lord of the Admiralty. If the mood of the little
gathering was sombre, there was ample reason. The Japanese had crossed the border of Burma the day before.
Rommel was, at that very moment, launching his counter-
attack in the Western Desert. There would probably be a
grave disturbance of public feeling if the Malaya campaign continued to go against the British as it was likely
to do. Churchill arrived in London to find newspapers
carrying without comment the statement from Sydney
that "if Singapore falls, Churchill will fall with it."

* The Cabinet Committee directly concerned with the conduct of
military operations. It included, among others, the Chiefs of Staff.

It was the opinion of Eden and Beaverbrook that, in these circumstances, the Government would be shaken. They remembered, no doubt, the ominous sentence in *The Economist* a fortnight earlier: "To beat General Rommel and lose Singapore would not only be disastrous; it would be nonsense; and it is wasted time for the authorities, in Britain or Malaya, to pretend there has not been miscalculation, as well as undoubtedly straitened resources and bad luck."

Nobody knew better than the members of the War Cabinet how vast the miscalculation had been, if indeed one can speak of "miscalculation" when there had been no calculation but rather, as it appeared, a dismissal from the mind of a problem which seemed to be insoluble and was certainly inconvenient.

Churchill, for his part, affected to be philosophically resigned to the prospect of public criticism and condemnation. A sense of the injustice of it all possessed him. Most of the Tory Party hated him, he said. He would be happy to leave office. The anxieties in Malaya, the intransigence of the Australians and the constant nagging in the House of Commons—it was more than any man could be expected to endure. He sought comfort for a moment in those self-indulgent dreams of power renounced and leisure recaptured which, in times of dejection, tempt the man of action.

But the dreams were dreams, and were quickly put aside. Churchill was, as statesmen must be, compounded of fine grain and not so fine. He was, at once, ruthless and emotional; sensitive to the feelings of others and capable, in moments of victory or anger, of a blind arrogance; happy in his personal life, yet basically lonely; wavering between the moments of abrupt decision and the long hours of doubt when he listened to too many counsellors and gave too much heed to the last. The memory of the

Dardanelles never left him, that prodigal child of his imagination whose ruin had been his own.

His complaint against the Australian Government was, surely, unreasonable. There were Australians lost in Greece, Australians in manifest danger on Singapore Island, Australians in Ceylon, Australian air squadrons of outstanding quality in Britain; all this at a time when every foundation on which Australian defence policy had been built seemed to be crumbling. Only two days distant in time was the Japanese seizure of Rabaul in New Britain, in the barrier of islands between Australia and the teeming, alarming continent of Asia. It was a moment when Curtin, the Australian Prime Minister, might have been excused for calling the legions home.

While Churchill was in Washington, Curtin had published an article in the *Melbourne Herald* in which he said: "We refuse to accept the dictum that the Pacific struggle must be treated as a subordinate segment of the general conflict. . . . Without any inhibitions of any kind, I make it quite clear that Australia looks to America, free of any pangs as to our traditional links with the United Kingdom." This inconvenient reminder that Australia was, after all, an independent nation caused Churchill not a little irritation. From Washington he instructed Attlee that there should be no "pandering" to it, and, writing about it later, he dismissed it as the "outpouring of anxiety".

In truth, the secret of Churchill's annoyance lay in the fact that his Middle East strategy, on which his ambition, his personal involvement and his kindled imagination were centred, largely turned on the magnificent fighting men of the Antipodes. Absorption in the personal duel with Rommel prevented him from feeling, as well as seeing, the realities of the Pacific, and he was slow to realize that the soldiers of the Australian Army were not, after all, his janissaries any more than the New Zealanders were.

The Australian newspapers should have helped him to a juster appreciation. As the Melbourne *Argus* fairly remarked: "Australians are right to insist that the mistakes of Greece and Crete should not be repeated in Malaya." Plainly, Curtin had his public behind him.

Generally speaking, however, Churchill had no reason to complain of the attitude of the public and the press during the days following his return from Washington. Imbedded in the warm blanket of the American alliance, the people nurtured a new-found confidence in victory and transmitted it, as *The Economist* noted, into a warm welcome for the leader whose spirit had kept them in the fight.

It is true that trouble for him lurked on the right wing of the Tory Party, which had never forgiven him his brilliance, his waywardness, his distant Liberal past. Some Tories had not forgotten Bonar Law's inveterate distrust of the man. There were even some premature essays in king-making. "The 1922 Committee [an important group of back-bench Conservative M.P.s] is understood to have selected Sir John Anderson as its candidate for the succession"[1] But if there was chatter in the lobbies of the House of Commons it did not go beyond that, and Sir John Anderson, an eminent, sententious administrator, was not a likely candidate for the throne should it ever become vacant. Of that there was no sign.

Mr. Churchill's deep hold on the mind and heart of the people was acknowledged by Harold Laski, who at the same time complained of his treatment of the House of Commons: "His relations with the House are those of a husband with a wife, who may speak freely at home but must not interfere with office matters."[2] In fact, while every aspect of Churchill's administration was sniped at by ill-tempered and, usually, inaccurate marksmen, he, the central figure, from whom all flowed and on whose judgment all depended, remained immune, the indispensable leader.

"Indispensable"? The adjective so profusely repeated may in time have come to fall with a disagreeable ring on Churchill's ear, especially when he noticed how often it served as the hypocritical prelude to some new attack on a trusted collaborator or on a course of policy which he had initiated. If he was Prime Minister, he meant to conduct the war himself, whatever others might say, and they said a great deal. "God knows," wrote Sir Alan Brooke, "where we should be without him, but God knows where we shall go with him." "It is such a pity," said Sir John Kennedy, Director of Military Operations at the War Office, "that Winston's fine courage and drive cannot be harnessed to the war effort in a more rational way."[3]

It had been so from the beginning. When Stanley Bruce (later Lord Bruce of Melbourne) told Beaverbrook in July 1940 that it would be disastrous if Churchill tried to run the war himself, Beaverbrook had answered: "Winston thinks he is a modern Marlborough."[4] And so it remained, for good or ill. For good *and* ill. Good because Churchill had ten times as much imaginative grasp as his military collaborators and most, at least, of his political associates. Ill because of his impatience and, in times of mental excitement, his inability to judge the relative quality of his own progeny of ideas. The lamp of genius burns with fitful brilliance.

In the three-day debate which opened in the House of Commons on Tuesday, 27 January, 1942, some of the worries besetting ordinary men and women came to the surface. Some but not all. Calamitous blunders had been committed, but they belonged to the past. What purpose did it serve to recall them? Ominous portents were in the heavens, visible to all. But the monstrous births had not yet taken place. They were not fit subjects for debate.

Churchill rose in a House, which, with all its galleries —studded with High Commissioners and peers, diplomats like Mr. Winant the American Ambassador and, "surprisingly" among the peers, the Crown Prince of Greece—was crowded but not overfriendly. By insisting on the discussion going forward under the shadow of a vote of confidence, the Prime Minister had made certain of an overwhelming victory in the division lobbies while arousing resentment among the Members.

After a friendly grin to Mr. Lloyd George, Churchill applied himself to the task of winning over his audience. Soon it was clear that he was in his craftiest and most captivating mood. Nobody, he said, need be mealy-mouthed in the debate or chicken-hearted in the lobby. On the critical issue of the Malayan defeats, no one was more accountable than he. Had it not been for him, there would have been a modern air force in that theatre, and tanks. But, three months before Japan broke into the war, the Caucasus was menaced; the Axis powers seemed to be bent on an east-and-west attack on the Nile Valley through Syria and Palestine on the one hand and from Libya on the other.

The spectre of this vast pincer-movement which haunted Churchill's strategy for so long (and which cannot be dismissed on the mere ground that it was never realized) had made it imperative to reinforce the Middle East "bastion", and to starve Malaya at a time when the Japanese attack was still problematical. And when that attack came the limiting factor in sending help had been, not shortage of weapons, but lack of shipping.

The news was bad and would get worse. There had been blunders and shortcomings, both in foresight and action. For these reasons, he said, "I demand a vote of confidence."

To so adroit and so unblushing a confession of guilt, the House of Commons responded like the fond wife of an errant but lovable husband. Mr. Erskine Hill, Chairman of the 1922 Committee, agreed that, if the Prime Minister insisted on his vote of confidence, he must have it, since nothing must be done to weaken his position in the world. There was, in fact, no doubt that Churchill would have his way.

The resumed debate revealed next day the sincerity and the confusion of the critics. One of the most effective of them was a Scottish Tory member, Sir John Wardlaw-Milne. After objecting that a vote of confidence would give the mistaken impression that the House was satisfied with the Government, he rejected the plea that the need to help Russia and strengthen the British forces in Libya was an adequate excuse for the meagreness of the defences in Malaya.

He found himself looking with amazement at the front bench, packed with ministers, unchanged after two years of war, still carrying on the same responsibilities as when they first took office. The Prime Minister was quite right, however, in accepting the sole responsibility. This was a dictatorship, with two dictators, one a deputy dictator dealing with the whole munitions problem—"two hearts that beat as one," said Sir John, in a sly reference to the relations between Churchill and Beaverbrook, which were too close for the liking of many, although not as complete as some people supposed. Sir John asked a question which was to become more and more familiar: "Proud as we are of the Prime Minister, is he not trying to do too much?"

Mr. Emanuel Shinwell, spry, belligerent and partisan, rose to speak in a different sense. This Glasgow Socialist who sat for Seaham Harbour was a master of Parliamentary tactics and an adept in the art of helpful opposition, prolific in useful diversions.

He would have been a member of the Government, if it had not been for an odd accident which happened at the time Churchill was picking his ministers in 1940. Shinwell was filling the chair at the Labour Party Conference when word was brought to him that the Prime Minister wanted to speak to him. He replied: "Impossible. Tell him I will ring at six." When he did so, Churchill asked him: "Will you speak for the Food Ministry in the Commons?" By this time Shinwell knew that Lord Woolton was Minister of Food; he was unwilling to act as Woolton's subordinate. When Churchill expressed his disappointment, Shinwell said: "I will do nothing to embarrass you; I am just as keen as you are to see the war vigorously prosecuted."

Apparently Churchill's first idea had been to make Shinwell his Minister of Shipping, a post he would certainly have accepted. But the plan miscarried. While Shinwell had spent the afternoon presiding over the party debate at Bournemouth, Dr. Hugh Dalton, his fellow-member on the Labour Party Executive, had been busy on the telephone to Attlee in London. The upshot of these activities had been that Sir Ronald Cross was moved to Shipping from the Ministry of Economic Warfare, which was then given to Dalton.

Shinwell, as a private Member of Parliament, filled a valuable, independent role as a well-informed and waspish critic of the Government, who never faltered in his conviction that Churchill was the best available war leader for the nation. To this role he brought talents which were not to be despised: cutting wit, cool logic, and a capacity to mould the minds of an audience to his pattern. Michael Foot, watching him from the Press Gallery, reported that his face "has the benevolence of a hawk and the sweetness of a vulture". There was, however, more sting than bitterness about Shinwell's Parliamentary performances. On

this occasion, he said slyly that it was unfortunate that
there could not be two votes of confidence: one in the
Prime Minister, the other in the Government.

Thus in Wardlaw-Milne's speech and in Shinwell's
the two main strands of criticism of the administration
were neatly juxtaposed. The one thought that an over-
worked Churchill should be relieved of half of his duties;
the other that the Prime Minister was impeded and embarrassed by the ineptitude of colleagues whose quality
was inferior to his own.

Sir Archibald Southby, Conservative Member for Epsom, put the crucial question: "The Government must
have been conscious all along of the deterioration in the
Far East. What did they do about it?" He was unlikely to
be satisfied with the answers he would be given. He threw
in the Government's face the sentence from the *Melbourne
Herald*: "The weakness and unpreparedness of the Empire's Pacific defences are to some extent due to the faults
of imperial strategy, bred of ignorance and prejudice."

Sir Percy Harris, a veteran Liberal Member, urged the
Prime Minister to divide his responsibility with other men.

That evening Lord Beaverbrook delivered a broadcast
which was, in effect, an intervention in the debate on
Churchill's side. He said: "We have many disabilities to
endure in this war. But [the] partnership [with the United
States] is a light in darkness, a comfort in gloom. It comes
directly from our own Prime Minister."

Some resentment might have been expected at the apparent way in which Beaverbrook had forced his way on
to the air to bring aid to a beleaguered Prime Minister.
But any such expectations proved to be unjustified. The
public took kindly to the display of chivalry, and so did
Churchill.

As soon as the broadcast was ended, the Prime Minister
telephoned to Beaverbrook to tell him how deeply

*Photo by Beaverbrook Newspapers*

The Prime Minister

*Photo by Keystone Press*

Lord Beaverbrook
on the day he joined the War Cabinet

touched he was by the words Beaverbrook had spoken.
He had heard them at a moment when he was meditating
resignation. In reply, Beaverbrook spoke words of comfort to Churchill: "Pitt was attacked more heavily than
you. Chatham had a worse time. Even Lloyd George in
the last war." So Beaverbrook, who had the reputation
of being the arch-resigner, argued with spirit and resource
against resignation.

But the incident had served to show that, in spite of his
extraordinary resilience, behind the buoyancy and the
cheerfulness, the Prime Minister was acutely sensitive to
the political perils of his position. Behind the front of resolution there lurked a self-questioning and doubting mor-
tal, a prey to the imagination that, simultaneously, fired
his spirit. It had been so before. After the debate on Norway in 1940, when a demonstration in the House had
made it impossible for Chamberlain to go on as Prime
Minister, Churchill had been summoned to Number Ten
to see Chamberlain and Lord Halifax. He went to the
meeting, expecting to be told that he could not succeed to
the throne that was being vacated. So small, at that moment, was the self-confidence of the man who, in the next
few weeks, was to steer Britain with strength and delicacy
through the greatest crisis in her history!

On the third and last day of the debate, 29 January,
1942, the Parliamentary storm lost a great deal of its fury.
Members had been persuaded that fate, not human failings, was at the heart of the strategic woes. The Prime
Minister had luck on his side when he rose to conclude the
debate: American troops had, two days before, landed in
Ulster. They would not, he said, do Mr. de Valera any
harm; they might do him some good. On the question of
the war in the Far East, he stood firm on his original argument, asking whether we ought in face of the Japanese
danger to have refused part of our aid to Russia. As for

Libya, it would remain a dangerous drain and a festering sore to the Axis powers.

Whether this was a complete and final statement of the position, the House had not the knowledge to judge. Nor had it the power, by cross-examining, to acquire that knowledge. It had received an account which, so far as it went, was candid and sensible. It was not in the mood to take the matter further. Deploying the mixture of humour and false humility which rarely failed to flatter the Members, the Prime Minister said he was much in need of the help of the House and ready to profit by its advice. He was not one of those saints who refused to do good because the devil prompted him. After these arch preliminaries, he said that he would soon appoint a Minister of Production. (Whispers reached the office of *The Times* that Beaverbrook would probably be chosen.)

After this, there was nothing to do but vote. By 464 to one (Mr. James Maxton), the Government's largest majority, the House of Commons decided to continue its confidence in Churchill and his Ministers. The figures did not tell the full story. Suspended judgments, stifled doubts and half-formulated misgivings—these did not appear in the division lists. *The Times* noted that Sir John Wardlaw-Milne's proposals represented the general feeling of the House.

The verdict of Parliament had, perhaps, been postponed. Shinwell quoted from Macaulay with cutting aptness: "Thus, through a long and calamitous period, every disaster that had happened outside the walls of Parliament has been regularly followed by a triumph within them." But, as Disraeli said, "a majority is always the best repartee." The Government lived to fight again.

Churchill took the opportunity to write to the leader of the Liberal Party, Sir Archibald Sinclair, a letter in terms that were sharp and—from one party leader to another

—verging on the impertinent. Pointing out that six Liberal M.P.s out of twenty had failed to vote in the vital division, he said: "I suggest to you that these matters require your very earnest consideration. . . . When its [the Liberal Party's] numbers are so small, it seems to me all the more necessary to have unity of action on occasions of confidence in the Government." Churchill, it has been said, was either on the heights or in the depths. On that day, he was on the heights, exulting in the sunshine of his Parliamentary triumph.

Next day, the rearguards of the British Army in Malaya crossed to Singapore Island. The causeway to the mainland was breached. The siege of Britain's great base in the Far East was about to begin. The omens were hardly propitious. *The Times* had, on the previous day, remarked casually that it could be no great secret that the defence of Singapore consisted entirely in preparations against an attack from the sea. The Japanese were about to launch their attack from the landward side.

There were unmistakable signs in London that, despite the vote of confidence, the political wind was still rising and was likely to reach gale force. *Tribune*, mouthpiece of Aneurin Bevan, left-wing Socialist member of Parliament, one-time associate of Stafford Cripps and inappeasable critic of the Prime Minister, appeared that Friday with the blunt challenge: "This is no national Government, and Churchill is no national leader." Lord Winterton, a highly respected Tory Member of Parliament, writing in the press, dismissed the absurd notion that the Government could be criticized apart from the Prime Minister. "The Prime Minister by his great position can win or lose this war. If the time ever comes when his methods are losing the war, it will be our duty to overthrow him."

# CHAPTER VII

## Site for a Shinto shrine

*An army can march anywhere and at any time of year wherever two men can place their feet.*
— Napoleon, *Military Maxims*

*A victorious army opposed to a routed one is as a pound's weight placed in the scale against a single grain.*
— Sun Tzu, *The Art of War*

SEVENTEEN DAYS AFTER the debate in the House of Commons, Singapore fell to the Japanese. An event so cruel to British pride and so shattering to the postulates on which British power was sustained, in the minds of strategists and laymen alike, demanded that some soothing and benumbing drugs should be administered. These were swiftly provided. Self-esteem is the most inventive of anaesthetists, the most co-operative of patients.

A picture was conjured up of numberless Japanese hordes, swarming through the jungles and drowning the defenders in a vast flood of fanatical warriors.[1] This was quite untrue. It was also said—as if it provided some excuse for the disaster—that nobody had ever contemplated a situation in which Singapore might be attacked from the north, over land. This again was untrue.

The number of Japanese troops engaged in the Malayan campaign seems never to have exceeded 60,000. The 25th

Japanese Army, which carried out the operation, consisted of three divisions, General Yamashita having decided in view of the poor morale which, as he had already discovered, existed among the defenders of Malaya, that a fourth division which had been made available to him was not needed.

Preparations for the invasion were marked by parsimony. Not for nothing was the Army Research Section which, during three hundred days of 1941, planned the invasion, known popularly among Japanese officers as the Doro Nawa unit, of which a rough equivalent is "the unit to make bricks without straw". A fund of 20,000 yen was earmarked to cover the expenses of research. With this modest sum an impressive task of fundamental military investigation into tactics, equipment, health,[2] topography and so forth was carried out.

It was all the more necessary because two of the divisions to be used in the invasion of tropical Malaya had been fighting in the sub-arctic conditions of Manchuria, while the third, the Imperial Guards, had not seen action as a unit since the Russo-Japanese war nearly forty years before. The Guards, although of exceptional physique, were haughty and elegant. They did not easily adapt themselves to the highly original and unorthodox methods of the campaign into which they were now to be plunged.

These methods had been tested—although not in jungle conditions—in the course of secret manoeuvres held in South China in June 1941; by the time the Japanese Army reached the Straits of Johore and was ready to make the final pounce on Singapore, their success was apparent to all.

However, it would be a complete mistake to suppose that the Japanese possessed some magical experience in jungle warfare, which the British, Indians and Australians had failed to acquire. Not one of the units of Yamashita's

25th Army had ever seen a jungle until it touched Malayan soil. In any case, most of the war was fought along the excellent roads of Malaya and not in its jungles.

What each Japanese soldier did possess was an intelligent doctrine governing the remarkable offensive on which he was embarked: the need to assert, to win, to strengthen and to maintain his moral ascendancy over an enemy whose will to fight was, at best, patchy; the need imposed by shortages of time, shipping and materials, to astound the foe with an unprecedented speed of manoeuvre and, travelling light, to live on the transport, food and fuel that was left behind by the enemy.

Each of the Japanese divisions was equipped with about 500 motor vehicles and 6,000 bicycles. Although only two or three months were available to accustom the troops to these new methods (in China, they had used horses), the training period proved to be long enough for tough and resolute men. When the bicycle tyres were punctured, the machines could be ridden on the rims when necessary so as to maintain the pace of the advance. On each coast of the peninsula, the Japanese employed light craft, mostly stolen from the British, in order to harass and threaten the enemy's flanks. These simple tactics had a remarkable degree of success.

In one important respect General Yamashita enjoyed overwhelming material superiority over his opponent: he had 617 aircraft at his disposal against a British strength of 141 serviceable aeroplanes at the opening of the invasion. Moral factors apart, this advantage was probably decisive.

On the ground, Yamashita had a larger number of tanks (about eighty) than General Percival, the British commander, who had only a single hastily-assembled squadron of light tanks from India. On the other hand, the British artillery was a more powerful force than the Japanese.

The Singapore base was four years old, almost to a day, when it was captured. Its official opening, on 14 February, 1938, came as the climax of a strident and prolonged campaign of publicity. The British public had been conditioned to believe that Singapore was "the most impregnable barrier on the waters of the world",[2] an "absolutely landlocked harbour", the huge and secret armament of which was protected by 800 feet of solid rock from any form of attack yet devised by man. Impressive details of the magnitude of the military works on which, it was said, more than £20 millions of the taxpayers' money had been spent, were allowed to find their way into print: twenty miles of railway, underground storage for one and a quarter million tons of fuel, a floating dock, a graving dock, etc.

"The Gibraltar of the East", as one enthusiastic journalist called it, seemed to be a new, almost impregnable bastion of Britain's imperial might in the East, 8,200 miles from England by sea. "It is now possible to say that the 'eastern frontier' of the British Empire is guarded by the greatest fortress in the world."[4] With such comforting sounds in his ears, the lion could stretch luxuriantly and fall asleep once more.

Amidst the festivities and splendours of the day when the graving dock was inaugurated in the presence of Mr. J. J. Llewellin, Civil Lord of the Admiralty, and 2,000 official guests, earlier doubts about the usefulness of the base were swept away. Yet doubts there had been. General Sir Ian Hamilton had said of the base: "I have no fears unless we ourselves fit out a halfway house and then —half-garrisoning it as is our wont—make a present of it

to the wrong people."[5] Admiral Dewar had called
Singapore "that white elephant" which, for its defence,
would require 30,000 men and an air force.[6]

But at such a moment of achievement there was no
time to recall misgivings of that kind. Nor does anyone
seem to have felt a prophetic twinge when his eyes fell
upon M. Okamoto, Consul-General of Japan, a lonely,
stocky figure, who stepped ashore from a destroyer and,
after spending the minimum amount of time at the opening ceremony, went home again as he had come, aloof,
alone. It did not seem to be M. Okamoto's day.

In that month of February 1938, the defences of Singapore were in the care of General W. G. S. Dobbie and
Air-Vice-Marshal Tedder. Combined exercises were held
by these commanders a few days before the opening of
the dock. They have some historical importance because,
as a newspaper report[7] stated at the time, defence headquarters based their plans on the assumption that the
main attack on the base would be launched against "the
back door", across the Straits of Johore, to the west of the
causeway linking the island to the mainland of Malaya.
The attacking troops would meet mangrove swamps, but
these, said the reporter with extraordinary prescience,
were much overrated as obstacles. The exercise of 1938
accurately prefigured the Japanese assault four years later.

So much for the legend that nobody had ever supposed
Singapore would be attacked from the rear.


When the Japanese assault was delivered on the night of
8 February, 1942, Lieutenant-General A. E. Percival, the
army commander on the island, had at his disposal a
total of 83,000 men, British, Australian and Indian, of
whom about 70,000 could be regarded as of combatant
status, armed and more or less trained. Some of the

soldiers were of better quality than others. Some had fought a two months' retreat down the peninsula, acquiring as they went an unhealthy respect for the fighting qualities of their adversary, his unconventional tactics, his determination and energy. Many of these defending soldiers were half-defeated before battle was joined. In other cases, the troops were only too new to the area. For instance, the Third Brigade of the 18th Division had come ashore as lately as 29 January, after a long sea voyage, and was unlikely to be in trim for action.

Nor was morale improved by the departure of the R.A.F. (saving a single fighter squadron) from Singapore to Palembang on the eve of the battle. The reason for this movement was simple and imperative: as soon as the Japanese were established on the Straits of Johore three of the four airfields on Singapore Island came under enemy gunfire. In the final stages of the encounter, the defenders of Singapore had no air support of any kind.

With his 70,000 men, General Percival's task was to defend a coastline eighty miles in length. In any normal conditions, the force should have been perfectly adequate. The circumstances were, however, not normal. The Straits of Johore divided an army supremely confident in its tactics and its leaders, exulting in a sustained and brilliant feat of arms which it was surely going to crown with a supreme triumph, from another army, somewhat more numerous, but haunted by a record of defeat, uncertain of the calibre of its commanders and penned in an island which had acquired strategic lustre as the base for a navy and which that navy had abandoned. It was unthinkable that Singapore should be given up without a fight—but what profit was there in defending it?

The first wave of the Japanese attack numbered 13,000 men, elements of two divisions who crossed in armoured landing craft (brought overland by road from

the west coast of Johore) at a point where the Straits of
Johore vary in width from 600 to 2,000 yards. They made
their way ashore after some hard fighting with the three
Australian battalions manning the sector. For some
reason, still unexplained, the beach searchlights were not
brought into use. Communication broke down. Intervention by the British artillery was slow. By dawn, most of
the 13,000 Japanese were ashore; before the day was over,
their numbers had swollen to 30,000, many of the later
arrivals swimming across with rifles and ammunition.

At sunset, General Yamashita and his staff crossed the
Straits on a raft made of three boats lashed together. By
dawn on 10 February he had established his command
post in a tent among the rubber trees.

On that day Churchill sent General Wavell, now
Supreme Commander in the Far East, a stern message:
"There must at this stage be no thought of saving the
troops or sparing the population. The battle must be
fought to the bitter end at all costs. . . . Commanders and
senior officers should die with their troops. The honour of
the British Empire and of the British Army is at stake."
The language was fierce and resolute but served only to
illustrate how utterly out of touch the writer was with
realities in Malaya. The months of inattention and half-
attention, of optimism and ignorance, could not be made
good by a burst of valiant rhetoric.

By nightfall on 11 February the crisis of the battle for
Singapore was over. General Yamashita sent a note to
General Percival: "Our counsel is that Your Excellency
will cease to think of meaningless resistance and from
now on, yielding to our advice, promptly and immediately
will suspend the action extending over the whole British
battle-front."

This advice was dropped from a reconnaissance aeroplane on the outskirts of Singapore city. It was taken on

15 February when a British major, carrying a large white flag of truce, appeared at half-past three in the afternoon before the lines of the 5th Japanese Division and received the terms of surrender. At six o'clock, General Percival met General Yamashita in the Ford car factory at Bikit Timah. Two hours and a half later, the war in Malaya was over. Singapore had fallen after a seven days' battle in which 1,700 Japanese were killed, almost half of the total losses in the campaign.

The Japanese staff sat down to an excellent table loaded with dried cuttlefish, chestnuts and wine, the gifts of their Emperor, who had sent an aide-de-camp with a rescript expressing his deep approval of the campaign. Facing in the direction of the imperial palace in Tokyo, the officers drank a toast to their fallen comrades. The smoke from blazing fuel-tanks darkened the sky. Looting Chinese and Malays were busy already among the European shops and dwellings of the city, which the conquerors ordained should thenceforth be known as Shonan. They removed the bronze statue of Sir Stamford Raffles and, with some care, chose the site for a Shinto shrine.

After 123 years, the most important British settlement in Asia had been captured and the greatest number of soldiers had capitulated in the whole of British history.

How had it happened?

Not, obviously, through any failure by the British Government to send a sufficient number of soldiers to Malaya. Was there not, indeed, a readiness to think too much in terms of numbers—so many "rifles, sabres, cannon", as Churchill loved to say? A mere piling up of military units does not solve a strategic problem, although it ministers powerfully to the peace of mind of a statesman 8,000 miles from the scene and grievously beset by nearer anxieties. Aircraft were a different matter. Strength in the air had not been sufficiently built up, and it is inaccurate to say that this reinforcement could not have been made. If Britain could spare 250 Hurricanes a month to Russia, could she not have diverted a comparable number to the Far East in the months immediately before the promise was given to reinforce the Russian air force?

In the period between January and July 1941, the Middle East theatre of war, which had a strength of thirty-five squadrons, received from Britain 1,300 aircraft. In the same period, Fighter Command in Britain had been built up to seventy-seven operational squadrons, and by October of that year Bomber Command had a strength of fifty-four squadrons and 955 aeroplanes. In the Far East, there were no more than twelve squadrons.

But, it will be objected, until 7 December, 1941, the Far East was not an active war zone. The threat was only potential. True. But in this case "potential" did not mean "possible"; it meant "probable". On no rational system of priorities can the distribution of British air power among the main theatres be defended.

As a consequence of these mistaken dispositions, the Japanese outclassed and overwhelmed the obsolescent R.A.F. fighters (Brewster Buffaloes) in the first hours of the assault on Singora (in Thailand) and Kota Bharu. The British air force was driven from its northern airfields in Malaya (which, incidentally, had no radar) so that when Admiral Sir Tom Phillips sailed the *Prince of Wales* and the *Repulse* out of Singapore to sink the Japanese transports, he knew that he would have no air cover and was liable to attack from Japanese torpedo bombers with an operational range of 500 miles. Nor did his fleet have any air cover from the navy, for the carrier *Hermes*, although in the Indian Ocean, had not been sent to join him. He went ahead with his plan—after all, was it to be supposed that he would abandon Malaya without a direct order from London?—although he was very soon aware that his fleet was being shadowed by Japanese aircraft. The tragedy that followed was, if not inevitable, at any rate highly probable.

Two capital ships, which had been designed, in the thinking of London, to serve as a vague threat to the enemy's sea communications, set off to interfere with his landing operations, which had already taken place and, while they looked for his transports, were destroyed.

The loss of the ships, added to the inadequacy of the air defences, made it almost impossible to hold Malaya against an attack of the weight, fury and originality of that mounted by the enemy. In due course, the loss of Johore made it impossible to defend Singapore. The defence of that island was contingent on the defence of Malaya as a whole. This in turn, depended on a group of airfields, which it was the role of the ground troops to protect. But, since those airfields housed a feeble obsolete and, soon, non-existent air force, the whole defensive scheme collapsed before it could operate. And the army was disposed on a strategic plan which was, from the beginning, meaningless.

Defective leadership? To what extent should that share in the blame for the catastrophe? General Percival was an officer of competence and courage, who completely lacked the dynamic qualities needed to grapple with a situation which was, from the beginning, desperate. He was, as Maurice Sarraut said of Gamelin, "a Berthier without Napoleon". Asked to play a role for which he was unsuited, he gave all that he could. It was not enough.

Had there been energetic preparation on the ground in Malaya and on Singapore Island—had tank obstacles and inundations been constructed—the Japanese advance might at least have been delayed. Had the troops been adequately trained in jungle warfare—which might have required a year—things might have been different. But this factor of jungle training should not be made to carry too heavy a burden of blame. After all, what sort of country is Malaya? Not a wilderness of swamp and jungle for the most part, but a highly developed peninsula with good roads which the Japanese used.

Had Wavell (who was always inclined to despise the Japanese) put in some ruthless, insistent man to organize the defence of the island, the final catastrophe might have been postponed. It could hardly have been averted. Indeed, it is the opinion of one competent authority, who knew Percival, the Japanese and the conditions of the Malayan fighting that, if Percival had been replaced by, say, Montgomery or Alexander, the campaign would have lasted only ten days longer. But undoubtedly a weak leadership must bear part of the blame for the peculiarly tragic nature of the catastrophe.

Where did the responsibility for selecting General Percival rest? Mainly with Sir John Dill, who had always thought highly of him. Thus it seems that Dill too, who believed that Singapore should rank ahead of Egypt in the order of priorities, had failed to measure the immensity of the crisis that would overtake Britain as soon as the Japanese launched their attack. He had chosen a competent staff officer for a command which called for a leader with fire in his belly and fury in his heart.


In the final assessment, the loss of Singapore was due to a total and many-sided miscalculation. The naval base had been called into being to give shelter to a fleet. But, in the event, there was not, there could not in the nature of things be, a fleet to shelter. For a fleet needs air cover and, when the crunch came, there were practically no aircraft.

Why then try to defend what was clearly indefensible? Had not Churchill been right when, awakening too late to the strategic realities of the Far East, he suggested on 20 January that Singapore could not be held and should, therefore, not be reinforced? The proposal was rejected, probably because of the fear of upsetting Australia. It should have been accepted. What purpose could be served in keeping an inadequate air force in the peninsula while reinforcing a considerable army which could neither fight successfully nor run away?

Singapore? The Japanese could either take the island or leave it, with the Union Jack flying over it, as the biggest prisoner-of-war camp on earth. They took it.


When Colonel Tsuji entered Singapore he was surprised to see that the British had not destroyed the airfields and harbour works. "Why did you not destroy Singapore?" he asked a young British officer. "Because we will return," the Englishman replied. "We may be defeated ninety-nine times, but the final round—that we will win."

After the Singapore disaster, the British had a score to pay off. In the unsparing battle of Imphal-Kohima in 1944 in which an Anglo-Indian-Ghurka army under General (later Field-Marshal) Slim met, out-fought and routed the Fifteenth Japanese Army, twice its number, the score was paid. Five Japanese divisions were destroyed and two mauled; 50,000 Japanese soldiers were killed; the total *irrecoverable* Japanese losses were 90,000, more than the total British losses at Singapore. The Japanese Army "suffered the greatest defeat in its history".[8]

After all, then, the final round was won—even if, in the light of future events, the victory may seem to have been somewhat pyrrhic.

# CHAPTER VIII

# *"The Government must break up"*

*War is a wasteful, boring, muddled affair; and people of fine intelligence either resign themselves to it or fret badly, especially if they are near the heart of things.*

—Lord Wavell

"THE LOSS OF AN ARMY IN SINGAPORE," wrote Aneurin Bevan, "is too high a price to pay for the education of a government."

Within nine days of the fall of the city there was a political crisis in London and a reconstruction of Churchill's administration. Yet, strangely enough, the disaster in the Far East was only one eddy in the disturbance of British opinion, and not even the strongest. It seems that the British people had, in their hearts, written off Singapore, at a time when the last ill-fated reinforcements were still arriving on the island. Parliament had debated the defeat before it happened and, while giving the Government a massive vote of confidence, had clearly reserved its final verdict on the conduct of affairs.

The Members were in an intricate dilemma: knowing more than they dared to utter, knowing less than they required to know if they were to frame and launch a comprehensive indictment, suspecting to the depths of their conventional, corporate soul the strange and wayward man who led them, wary of the brilliance that dazzled them and the oratory that cast its spell, longing perhaps for the return of someone of their own stature.

They were a popular assembly, with the weaknesses of their kind, as jealous of their rights as a slighted wife, as resentful of the wheedling arts of genius as a ploughboy duped at the fair.

These irritations were all the harder to bear because they knew that Parliament, the sovereign body, enjoyed something less than its normal authority. It was six years and four months old, and, in the ordinary course of events, the legal term of a Parliament is five years. It might be true, as A. P. (later Sir Alan) Herbert claimed, that there were 170 new faces in the House since the general election and nearly eighty since war began.[1] But the political ingredients were fixed by a war-time party truce in the pattern of 1935, and such symptoms as could be discerned did not encourage members to think that they represented any longer what the people of Britain felt. There were indications that the long-delayed swing of public opinion away from the Conservative Party was beginning; in a few weeks, those indications would be more marked.

In truth, the world to which the 1942 House of Commons belonged and which it represented was already dead. It had been destroyed, like the old European system, by the triumph of Hitler and by the failure of pre-war governments to defeat him. No doubt those governments and the Parliaments to which they were answerable had given the people what it wanted, a postponement of the inevitable. But the sovereign people, like other sovereigns, is under no obligation to be grateful to a servant who has failed through excess of faithfulness.

In 1941–2, the House of Commons did not fully understand, although some portions of it might suspect, that it, and all that it stood for, belonged to a world of shadows. The Labour Party, shuddering with embarrassment, tried to forget its own record of futility in the years of appeasement. Among the Conservatives, the pro-Chamberlain and pro-Eden factions of the days of the Abyssinian war still snarled at one another. Should anything happen to Winston Churchill, "which Heaven forbid", many would be for Anthony Eden; the official Conservative view might be for Kingsley Wood; a fair-sized section would press for David Margesson. This, at any rate was the view of Beaverbrook,[2] who realized that a great gulf had opened between the House of Commons and the country.

But, obsolete or not, men's duty as Members of Parliament remained, to approve the Government or to replace it. In February 1942, at a crisis of the war, they could bring themselves to do neither.

Four days before the collapse at Singapore, the German battle cruisers *Scharnhorst* and *Gneisenau*, along with the cruiser *Prinz Eugen*, which had been lurking at Brest for nearly a year, made their way safely back to Germany through the Straits of Dover. The escape was all the more galling for the public since, for some hundreds of miles, the ships were sailing within easy range—sometimes within actual sight—of the English coast and were attacked constantly, valiantly and ineffectively by shore-based aircraft and destroyers. The incident was in dismal contrast to the successful Japanese air attack on the *Prince of Wales* and the *Repulse* two months earlier. "Vice-Admiral Ciliax has succeeded," said *The Times* caustically, "where the Duke of Medina Sidonia failed."

The credit, in fact, belonged to Hitler himself who had insisted on the exploit and, in the euphoria that it produced, listened with more sympathy than usual to his Grand Admiral Raeder. This strategist had devised a

"Great Plan" for a German air and military offensive in the Mediterranean which, coupled with the anticipated Japanese domination of the Indian Ocean, would starve the British out of the Middle East. The key to the Great Plan was to be the seizure of Malta. In the afterglow of *Scharnhorst* and *Gneisenau*, Hitler allowed preparations for this project to begin.

The strategic effect of the escape of three German ships was, at first, exaggerated in Britain. It seemed that the Germans would now have at their disposal six heavy ships with screening craft, a force capable of doing a great deal of mischief on the Atlantic shipping lanes. What if they were to seize Iceland? wondered the more pessimistic newspaper strategists. In that event, the whole situation in the Atlantic would be gravely transformed. It turned out, however, that the escaping ships had been seriously damaged during their voyage and were not likely to give much trouble for some time.

Compared with the military catastrophe in the Far East, the affair of the warships was an annoying minor setback. It was not seen in that light by the public. "A sort of shudder of horror passed over Britain today," reported Robert B. Post to the *New York Times*. Britain's blind faith in its command of the sea "rocked to its foundations. Britons question their government as never before."

Gravely reviewing the events of "the worst week we have passed through since the fall of France," *The Spectator* noted that the escape of the ships was "a blow which has shaken the average Briton more than any other". This fairly represented the exasperated and ill-proportioned public temper of the moment, which found acid expression in the newspapers that week—the "crabs", as Churchill called them; or "Quislings", to use the name preferred by Ernest Bevin.

"We are glad," said the leading article in the *Daily Mail* of 18 February, "that Mr. Churchill has instituted an enquiry into the failure to intercept the German warships. Public anger and disquiet were particularly aroused over this episode because people felt that it was symptomatic. They do not ask for scapegoats, but they do feel that something is very definitely wrong at the top." Political conclusions were drawn. While the *Evening News* challenged Churchill's war strategy, the *Daily Herald* was "apprehensive", and *The Spectator* acknowledged that "the Churchill difficulty deepens".

The Prime Minister himself had emphasized it by asking the House of Commons to realize the enormous burdens falling on him not as Minister of Defence but by his constant attendance on the House. Of these duties, said *The Spectator*, Lloyd George had been relieved by Bonar Law. "Who could fill that role adequately today?" It suggested Mr. Eden. *The Times* (18 February) said that "a large body of patriotic and entirely friendly opinion is urging Mr. Churchill to accept some relief".

*The Economist* (21 February) thought that, for the first time since he took the helm, the Prime Minister did not understand the people. He drew a picture, by implication, of a perfectly designed government machine running at half speed because it was insufficiently fuelled by the efforts of the people. Wholly false! Now a "catalogue of catastrophes" had produced a political crisis.

"We do not believe the people want to lose Mr. Churchill. We do not believe they would let him go." But manifestly wrong were the military conduct of the war, the lack of decision in Whitehall, the continued presence in the War Cabinet of men of less than the highest competence.

There was a need to replace these men of sixty with the men of forty—"the generation that has produced the

Nazi planners and the brilliant Soviet generals". There
was need for a real War Cabinet of men free and able to
decide: Cripps, Bevin, Beaverbrook ("whose energy out-
weighs his defects"), Eden, Sir John Anderson, Oliver
Lyttelton.

The recipe offered by Aneurin Bevan's *Tribune* (20
February) was more summary: "We visualize a Government in which Churchill is still Prime Minister but not
Minister of Defence." The trouble was that Churchill had
known just such a Government, and he remembered what
had happened to its Prime Minister, Mr. Asquith. He had
been supplanted by Mr. Lloyd George.

An unsuccessful war. An over-burdened Prime Minister.
A nation weary of failures. A confusion of counsellors.

Some, like Sir William Beveridge and *The Economist*,
argued in favour of a small War Cabinet of men whose
minds were free of departmental responsibility; others for
a Deputy Prime Minister who would relieve Churchill of
the Parliamentary duties he felt most onerous. Others
again asserted that, since the main failure lay in the realm
of higher strategy, this task should be taken over by a
Minister of Defence who would not be Prime Minister.
It was the most logical solution and the least likely to be
accepted.

For, as Beaverbrook said,[3] this was Churchill's war.
His was the guiding hand and he would—whatever he
said—willingly share the helm with nobody. Yet something must be done to appease the storm.

"For the first time since Winston Churchill became
Prime Minister, millions of Britons last week began seriously to question his abilities." Thus the situation was
summed up by American observers, surveying the scene
with a friendly but dispassionate eye.[4] "Have we not been

hypnotized by Mr. Churchill's personality, by the force
of his rhetoric, by his hold on the House of Commons?
Have we not been drugged . . .?" the *News Chronicle*
wondered plaintively.

It was apparent in these conditions that some scrap
must be thrown to the "crabs". Cripps must be harnessed.
Some of the fading flowers in the Cabinet should be put
reverently in the dustbin. Above all, war production,
about which there was so much half-informed grumbling,
fed by rumours from the forces and the factories, must
be re-arranged. The task was more difficult than it looked.
Plans for new and improved dispositions could be drawn
up. No trouble about that. But personalities were the real
key and they were strong and rebarbative.

Above all, there were Bevin and Beaverbrook, men of
exceptional quality, possessing, the one in his command
of the trade-union movement, the other in his newspapers
and in the lustre of his achievement as supplier to the
Battle of Britain, sources of power independent of their
places in the Government. They were, in truth, two of the
great feudatories of the realm. The relations between
these two powers were correct but prickly. Bevin distrusted Beaverbrook, an "anarchist"; Beaverbrook found
Bevin too rough for his liking, a boor.

Bevin had derived from his trade-union past an in-
grained respect for the letter of an agreement, the agenda
of a committee, the democratically appointed chairman
of a party. Characteristic of him were his relations with
Attlee, leader of the Parliamentary Labour Party. "How
are they?" asked Halifax of those relations. "Oh, very
good indeed," replied Beaverbrook, "like two high and
distant mountain peaks, each with snow on it."[5] But this
was hardly the full picture.

Bevin had a kind of contemptuous affection for Attlee,
a man with a genius for being underrated (by Churchill,

Beaverbrook, Halifax, etc.); yet with this was combined a genuine respect for the legal democratic authority which Attlee embodied. In Beaverbrook, respect for authority was weak; far stronger was his impulse to personal loyalty. Bevin and Beaverbrook conceded each to the other a reluctant respect, tinctured with dislike. Bevin would probably have agreed with Halifax's judgment on Beaverbrook; "Like all people of that sort, he only begins to listen if you contradict him flat."⁶

But so long as Bevin was Minister of Labour, heaven-appointed protector of the organized workers, and as jealous of his rights as any legitimist, while Beaverbrook was the Minister of War Production designate in Churchill's mind, fences between them must be mended, duties must be defined and boundaries must be marked out.

To this task of appeasement Beaverbrook had, in fact, been applying himself, for six months or more, perhaps under stimulus from Churchill. The results had not been encouraging.

Bevin thought that Beaverbrook, while Minister of Supply, had used his influence with the press to obtain unfair advantages for himself in matters like the allocation of labour. There had been a stormy scene between the two men one July day in 1941 in the office, normally the Chief Whip's, which Beaverbrook retained at Number 12 Downing Street. It ended when Beaverbrook, exasperated by Bevin's truculence, protested vehemently: "But I have told my papers to play you up, Ernie. I look on you as the leader, the Prime Minister, if Churchill goes!" Bevin had replied, "Max, you ought to be secretary of the Cabinet-makers' Union." It was doubtful whether Beaverbrook's protestation could be taken at its face value and more doubtful still that Bevin believed it.

Even after this outburst, the unhopeful courtship went

on for another ten days and broke down—finally, as it seemed—over a difference of opinion on the recruiting of Ministry of Supply factories in Lancashire.

Beaverbrook wrote to say that he would find the workers himself since Bevin had failed to do so. Bevin's reply was rude. It seemed that he was resolved not, at any price, to succumb to the other man's legendary charm or to the well-simulated tantrums with which, when all else failed, he would try to get his way in Cabinet. It was certain that Beaverbrook could not obtain from Bevin by an exercise of *force majeure* what persuasion would not give him.

As the autumn of 1941 rolled by, Beaverbrook, feeling himself at the apex of his power in the country, was keeping alive a series of grievances against his colleagues. With the Secretary of State for Air, Sir Archibald Sinclair (later Lord Thurso), he had a dispute over aircraft which must be sent to Russia under the agreement he had made with Stalin. He had fallen out with Eden, who had refused to let him see a letter from Sir Stafford Cripps criticizing the Beaverbrook mission to Moscow. He was angry with the Chief of the Imperial General Staff, who was making difficulties over the supply of tank spares to the Russians. He was conducting a running fight with Bevin over manpower. He thought that Churchill should do more to take German troops from Stalin's back by creating a major diversion in the West. And, as if all these troubles were not enough, he was engaged in an acrimonious controversy with the Petroleum Board, who wished to prevent him from winning possession of the top storeys in Shell-Mex House for his Ministry of Supply which occupied the rest of the building.

Among these annoyances, great and small, the dispute with Bevin bit by far the deepest. It had the quality of a personal duel between two powerful, cunning and ambitious fighters, Retiarius wielding a net, Secutor armed with a club. The bitterness and irritation which it engendered were, it seems, often at the root of Beaverbrook's assertion, made more than once and with a notable disregard for the ears that might hear, that he meant to leave the Government—or, at least, the War Cabinet.

During the last days of October 1941, some London newspapers published a report that Lord Beaverbrook was suffering from ill-health and that his early resignation might be expected. Churchill was perturbed by the interpretation given to these rumours by the foreign press, which alleged that the real reason for Beaverbrook's departure, if it occurred, would be his disagreement with his colleagues over help for Russia. Lord Halifax sent the Prime Minister a personal telegram from Washington: Harriman had telephoned him to say that the news of Max's contemplated resignation were being used to make mischief. Churchill, in a meeting at Number 10, urged the Minister to deny the rumours. About the same time came a message from Stalin to Churchill, declaring that Lord Beaverbrook must stay in the Government so that Russia could be confident that deliveries of armaments he had promised to her would be made.

The storm passed. Churchill wrote to Beaverbrook a letter breathing affection and concern for his friend who was, he could see, overwrought and tugged at by conflicting emotions and influences. "I wish," said the Prime Minister, "you would be as wise a counsellor to yourself as you have so often been to me."[7] The appeal, so movingly and dexterously addressed to its audience, had an instant effect.

Beaverbrook had on the previous night volunteered to go to Moscow as Ambassador, retreating eastwards if need be, with the Russian armies and Government. He believed that Cripps was making ready to return to

London, with the intention of assuming the leadership of the Opposition. The evidence for this surmise was slight, although sufficient for a man with an acute insight into the springs of political conduct: Cripps from Kuibyshev had complained that Beaverbrook, by excluding him from the political talks at Moscow, had impaired his prestige with the Russians, who no longer believed he had any very high standing with the British Government.

On receiving Churchill's appeal, Beaverbrook withdrew his resignation. The effect on the Prime Minister's spirits was immediate. It was sunshine after shadow.

No more was heard of the proposal that Beaverbrook might go to the Moscow Embassy. And very soon he was casting his eye in the direction of Washington, where he thought he might play a useful ministerial role in co-ordinating the war production of the United States and Britain. In any case, more could be done in Washington than in Moscow by a pertinacious and determined friend who wished to help the Russians.

However, the feud in the Cabinet over production dragged on into the winter months. Several expedients were thought of to end it. Could it be resolved by making Beaverbrook the overlord of all war production, with a new Minister of Labour congenial to him? Sir Walter (later Lord) Citrine, perhaps? This—apart from Citrine's own views—would depend on Bevin's willingness to leave the post at the Ministry of Labour which he regarded as his by divine right. And what other Ministry could be found acceptable to the mighty saurian?

With the spread of the war to the United States and Japan, the troubles in the British Government were suspended rather than resolved. Beaverbrook did not carry out his frequently stated intention of leaving the Ministry of Supply on 1 January. (On that day he was carrying out

crucially important talks in Washington.) By the first
week of February 1942, the Prime Minister approached
the intractable problem of organizing production, the
core of which, as he could see, lay in the difficult personal
relations between Bevin and Beaverbrook.

He proposed to invite them to dinner at Chequers together so that their differences could be composed in a
genial after-dinner glow. Whether this was a good idea
may be doubted. Beaverbrook regarded war-time
Chequers as a chilly mansion where the food was not very
good. In the meantime new occasions of annoyance had
arisen.

Eden accused Beaverbrook of inciting the *Daily Express*
to attack his foreign policy. Beaverbrook thought that he
detected the hand of Bevin behind a leading article in the
*Daily Herald* in which he was criticized. He wrote a note
and thought of passing it across the Cabinet table to the
Foreign Secretary: "This Government is Bedlam. You
accuse me of attacking you in the *Express*. Bevin writes
leaders against me in the *Herald*. The Government must
break up."

The article in the *Herald* which annoyed Beaverbrook
appeared at the moment when Churchill had taken the
plunge and announced Beaverbrook's promotion to be
Minister of Production, a promotion accepted with every
sign of reluctance: "He is to be tried out," the *Herald*
wrote, "in an office which—we quote the Prime Minister
—requires a combination of the qualities of Napoleon
and Christ. Frankly, Lord Beaverbrook falls short of that
requirement." After this astringent opening, the writer
moved swiftly on to disclose where his real interest in the
business lay. "The Ministry of Labour," he said, "has
provided the men and women faster than our industrial
organization could employ them . . . what we hope from
Lord Beaverbrook is that he will turn, at last, to full

account the energies of the men and women who are being faithfully supplied by the Ministry of Labour."

Here, in the most forthright terms, was a warning to the new overlord of war production: Keep out; do not interfere.

The reorganization of the Government was, in truth, unsatisfactory. Cripps, approached to become Minister of Supply, refused to serve under Beaverbrook. As the intention was that the new Minister of Production should be in control of priorities and the allocation of raw materials, Cripps could not see that the Minister of Supply, whoever he was, would be any better able than before to increase production. Besides, Beaverbrook was apparently about to make a prolonged visit to the United States; who would carry on the Ministry of Production in his absence?

The Prime Minister, to whom these objections were stated, replied in terms which suggested that, in his view, the overriding necessity was to appease Lord Beaverbrook by finding him "a new tremendous sphere where the irritation any kind of obstruction raised in him would be at its minimum". The strange argument was not calculated to make much appeal to Cripps, or to Bevin either.

The Minister of Labour, for his part, made it clear that the realm of production would be a dual monarchy—and that he distrusted his fellow sovereign. "By nature," said *The Economist* of Beaverbrook,[8] "he is a 'partisan', a guerrilla. He will not sit easily in the seat of judgment with no axe to grind." A Minister of the temperament and reputation of Mr. Oliver Lyttelton would have been a better choice. *The Spectator* was no less dubious of the new arrangements: "Lord Beaverbrook will have the whip-hand over the production departments by controlling supplies of materials; Mr. Bevin, by controlling supplies of manpower. This is a duality which will demand ideal compatibility of temperaments between Lord Beaverbrook and Mr. Bevin: We can only pray that grace will be bestowed on both of them."

Something more than grace was needed, an exceptional degree of good luck amounting almost to the miraculous. And this was denied, even in small things.

Friends of the two men, who thought that the feud between them was doing injury to the national cause, made an effort at reconciliation through Mr. (now Sir) Trevor Evans, industrial correspondent of the *Daily Express*, who knew both Ministers intimately and enjoyed their confidence. Evans suggested to Beaverbrook, who adopted the idea with alacrity, that Bevin should be invited to dinner at Cherkley. When the invitation was put to Bevin he regarded it at first with deep suspicion, but accepted when he was assured that loyal friends of his were behind the proposal.

"Can I bring Flo?" asked Bevin. Mrs. Bevin was, of course, welcome.

Evans arrived at Cherkley an hour before the Bevins were due. Beaverbrook received them with all the social grace of which he was master. Conversation in the salon opened amicably if cautiously. Evans went out of the room to make, at Beaverbrook's request, a telephone call to the *Sunday Express* office. It was, perhaps, injudicious of Beaverbrook to disclose to Bevin that he was in communication with his newspapers. But can it be wondered at if, at times, he cast a regretful, backward glance at Fleet Street? He had so much to share, he would have been more than human if his hand had not hovered sometimes over the telephone. The path of a newspaper-magnate turned statesman is strewn with pebbles of frustration.

After an absence of about six minutes, Evans returned to find that the situation was dramatically changed. The Bevins were leaving! Somewhat out of countenance,

Beaverbrook was following them to the front door. "Sorry you can't stay to dinner," he said.

When the guests had departed, Beaverbrook said to Evans: "All the more for you and me, Trevor." Later, during the meal, he said: "These fellows in the Labour party will have to develop a better sense of humour if they are ever going to succeed. They are far too touchy."

As far as Evans was able to reconstruct the happenings during his absence, Bevin had said, "This is a nice place you have here," with a wave of the hand towards the superb view from the Cherkley windows. "Yes," Beaverbrook answered jokingly, "and I expect you fellows will take it away from me some day."

At this, Bevin flew into a sudden rage: "Come on, Flo. I won't stay here and have the Labour cause insulted."

Weeks later Evans heard Bevin's account of the incident: "He was very offensive. I won't listen to anybody who regards the Labour party as confiscators." It was substantially the same story as Beaverbrook's.

One Saturday, at a time when the crisis between the two ministers was approaching its peak, Lord Beaverbrook resolved to make a supreme effort at reconciliation. He invited "Ernie" to lunch in his private dining-room at the Ministry of Supply in Shell-Mex House. Everything was arranged between the two batteries of private secretaries for lunch on Sunday at one. Then it was discovered that Lord Beaverbrook had a meeting with the tank experts at that time. One of his private secretaries resolved the dilemma, putting the tank men's appointment forward by half an hour and Mr. Bevin's back by half an hour. All was well? Alas! During the night the secretary awoke in alarm: he had forgotten to warn Lord Beaverbrook's valet, Albert, whose task it would be to provide and serve the meal. In the early hours of Sunday this omission was made good.

The last obstacle was surely surmounted. No! For Mr.

Bevin's secretary forgot to tell *him* of the change of time.
For half an hour the Minister of Labour kicked his heels
at Shell-Mex House waiting for his host with what
patience he could muster.

The rivalry between the two champions remained; its
effect was to deprive of all credibility the united control
over the industrial front.

"Lord Beaverbrook," said *Tribune*,[10] which was singu-
larly well-informed about the new Minister's private
thoughts, "is a Minister of Production in name only."

In these conditions, was it likely, or even conceivable,
that Churchill's re-shuffle could be made viable? In fact
the real collapse of the scheme occurred on the same day
as it was made public in Parliament. Churchill was, at that
time, in a state of nervous tension, feeling in advance the
shock of Singapore. Bevin had formed an alliance with
Cripps against Beaverbrook.

The White Paper defining the tasks of the various production authorities did not satisfy Beaverbrook, who felt
that he was asked to supervise the supply ministries without being master of the ministers.

He resigned one night—and decided next morning (10
February) that, at so late an hour, he had no alternative
but to accept the White Paper. By eleven a.m. he must
answer "yes" or "no". In a final outburst of annoyance,
he protested: "This ultimatum is all damned nonsense."

At two minutes to eleven he threw the White Paper on
the desk saying: "There is your answer."

"He can publish?" asked the Prime Minister's representative.

"Yes," said Lord Beaverbrook.


What was "settled" in such a spirit was not likely to survive for long. And so, nine days later, a second re-shuffle

of ministers occurred. Beaverbrook, who had so often resigned, resigned. On earlier occasions Churchill had declined his friend's resignation. "People don't resign in war-time," he said. "You either die or are sacked." This time he accepted it.

In the second re-shuffle, Cripps became Leader of the House of Commons and a member of the War Cabinet; Oliver Lyttelton (a Conservative M.P. who had been Minister of State in the Middle East; a man of high ability, wit and distinction) took over the post that Beaverbrook had momentarily filled at Production. It could be regarded as a victory for Bevin and his new ally Cripps.

Mr. A. J. Cummings, the leading Liberal journalist, found "a certain irony in the fact that the one man, apart from the Prime Minister, whose driving power and capacity for getting things done commanded general confidence now drops out".[11] Not many people realized that Beaverbrook's brusque Canadian voice was one of the few that Churchill would listen to when in the headlong flight of his imagination. When that voice could no longer be raised in Downing Street, a salutary corrective and cautioner was removed.

As for the public, stunned by the "catalogue of catastrophes" in the field, it was comparatively unmoved by the astonishing political double somersault that had taken place. On the whole, the general opinion was that the Government had on balance been strengthened. The departure of Beaverbrook was held to be more than counterbalanced by the arrival of Cripps—embodiment of a new, sterner spirit and, as *Tribune* said, "a symbol of our close alliance with Russia". *The Times* detected a changed mood in the land, with firm backing for the Government. Even Cummings, while mourning the departure of Beaverbrook, announced that in Cripps Parliament had found a new leader and a new inspiration.

*Photo by Radio Times Hulton Picture Library*

Ernest Bevin as Minister of Labour addressing factory workers with a "Bevin Beauty" at his side

*Photo by Photographic News Agency*

Winston Churchill and Lord Beaverbrook
in informal conference

This comforting thought was widely shared among Members of Parliament of all parties who had been deeply impressed by a speech delivered by Cripps to an overflowing meeting of the Inter-Parliamentary Union. "Young M.P.s agreed that they had never heard anything like it" (*The Star*); "far from being the cold, impersonal speech of a lawyer," said the *Evening Standard*, while the *Daily Telegraph* coldly remarked, "he read practically every word".

Conservatives said to one another afterwards that, if anything were to happen to Churchill, here in Cripps they had found his successor. It was an ironic tribute to one whom the German newspapers were calling "the execrable Cripps, the salon Bolshevist".

But not everybody agreed with these high opinions. While the issue was still being decided, Beaverbrook opposed the appointment of Cripps as Leader and, with Eden's approval, pressed the claims of Eden to the post. Churchill was doubtful: "You are a doer, not a talker," he said to Eden.[12]

The chief Conservative Whip, Mr. James Stuart (now Lord Stuart of Findhorn), argued in favour of Cripps who, being unpopular with Labour, would be the more likely to appeal to the Tories. And in the end Cripps it was.

A few days later, the new Leader, in a speech which *The Times* called "invigorating", was informing the House of Commons that the people wished to treat "this grave situation with all the seriousness and austerity it undoubtedly demands". In Berlin, Goebbels rejoiced: "Cripps is Stalin's messenger in London . . . a propaganda argument . . . It is good for our people, it is good for our allies, it is good for the neutrals and it is fateful for our enemies."[13]

A new chapter in the war had opened. The State was re-dedicated to asceticism. Simultaneously a parallel change occurred at the peak of the Anglican establishment. On

23 February, Lord Halifax mused in his diary: "So Willie Temple is Cantuar. I am very pleased."

Beaverbrook wrote "My dear Winston" a generous and touching letter of farewell which pleased the Prime Minister greatly. "I like him very much," he said.

"With a stroke of the pen, Max has won back all the lost ground," Sir Charles Wilson (later Lord Moran) observed; he had noticed that "a difference of opinion with the President or Max Beaverbrook took more out of him [Churchill] than a major disaster in the field".[14]

Refusing the offer of a Government post in Washington, Beaverbrook agreed with the Prime Minister's suggestion that his withdrawal from the Ministry could be attributed to ill-health. Soon he regretted that he had done so.


Why, it may be asked, did Beaverbrook, a man who took just pride in the staunchness of his friendships, who certainly had no fear of the storm, quit Churchill's Government in that black week of February 1942?

The official explanation, that his health had broken down, that he was a victim of asthma, was widely believed at the time.

Lord Moran, who at that time knew as much about Beaverbrook and his health as he knew about Churchill's, thinks otherwise. Beaverbrook, he says, aware of the dislike which some other ministers felt for him, had lost faith in himself: "It was his own profound distrust in himself that haunted him in office. If he found that he was not up to his job, he must get out of it before he made some disastrous mistake."[15] Lord Beaverbrook's asthma was, he thinks, a symptom of nervous strain rather than an independent ailment.

This may be, and it is certain that Beaverbrook had

spent himself more lavishly than was normal in a political chief on the work of his Ministry. After months of passionate labour, he was a tired man and, perhaps, unusually open to the invasion of self-doubt. Especially in the period before and during the Battle of Britain, he had assumed a triple burden—of sheer physical labour, of sustained mental exertion testing even to a man of his abnormally robust intellect, and of high-pitched nervous strain, for he was not one of those who remain serene in the fight. In addition, there was an emotional involvement— his son was a pilot taking part, day after day, in the Battle. The ordeal would have broken many a man; it made Beaverbrook's asthma more acute.

The nervous exhaustion may be admitted, but self-distrust, the explanation which Lord Moran proposes, remains no more than speculation. Lack of self-confidence had not previously been a conspicuous feature of Lord Beaverbrook's temperament. It is significant, surely, that at this time he was actually seeking more authority than others were prepared to concede to him.

Sir Archibald Rowlands had a more plausible explanation when he told Captain Liddell Hart[16] that Beaverbrook thought the administration was losing ground and did not want to be involved in its collapse. It is certain that Beaverbrook did not at any time like to be associated with failure, especially when the failure was not one of his making. Anything of the sort seemed to him an act of injustice which caused him real misery and annoyance.

The war, as he said to Liddell Hart a month after he had left the Government, was Churchill's war, conceived by him in terms of the wars of Marlborough.

"With a tinge of the nineteenth century?" Liddell Hart suggested.

"More than a tinge."

Beaverbrook had been at variance with Churchill on

such major issues of war policy as the diversion of important war supplies to the Middle East in 1940, the Greek escapade in 1941, and, later, when he was more disposed than the Prime Minister to fall in with Stalin's wishes, military help to Russia. But Singapore was the great failure which coincided with Beaverbrook's departure from the Government; and Singapore was not one of the issues on which he disagreed with the Prime Minister. Beaverbrook's opinion was that the failure in Malaya was human in origin and not material or strategic, caused by a breakdown in morale and leadership rather than a shortage of equipment. He was inclined to blame Sir John Dill and not the Prime Minister.

In any case, he can hardly have supposed that, by detaching himself from the Government after the disaster occurred in the Far East, he would escape from the general responsibility and odium which followed it.

It seems more likely that Beaverbrook acted under a compulsive yearning to resign of which nervous exhaustion was only one element. He could see no means of exerting a real formative influence on strategy against a masterful Prime Minister, who was his personal friend. He had become irritated by Churchill's "endless monologues" in Cabinet. He was, within reasonable limits, a hedonist and the absence of boredom was a pleasure he particularly cherished.

He had, moreover, information from medical sources about the Prime Minister's health of which he took an unduly pessimistic view. Churchill, it was said, had suffered a heart attack in Washington. The possibility that Britain at the crisis of the war, might suddenly be deprived of her leader was a factor that could not be overlooked. Would it not be a real service to the country if there was a respected figure in reserve? The question may well have been present in Beaverbrook's mind.

But, it seems, the basic cause of his resignation was his temperamental antipathy to Ernest Bevin, which assumed exaggerated dimensions in the imagination of a weary man. He could not be, as he wanted to be, sole dictator of war production. Bevin's veto prevented it. And he could not divide the kingdom with the rival.

He could not be master; he had no faith in a partnership.

## CHAPTER IX

# *"I, Churchill, will serve you"*

*I never met him but with pleasure, and never left him but with regret.*
—General John Fitzwilliam on Horace Walpole

ON 24 FEBRUARY, a week after making the changes in his Government, Churchill dined with his old friend Beaverbrook. Outside, the weather was bitterly cold. It was the unusually long winter of which, even a month later, Joseph Goebbels was writing irritably in his diary: "Will this winter never end?"[1] It was the winter that saved Russia.

In the warmth of the dining-room, the emotional temperature was high. Churchill later called it "the most painful evening in my life". Affection; regret; a renewal of doubts; memories; some remorse—all of these made their contribution to the atmosphere at the encounter.

The Prime Minister had just won a spectacular Parliamentary victory; he enjoyed an unprecedented measure of popular support.[2] He did not overrate the value of either. The sullen approval which the House of Commons gave him could, in a moment, flare into rebellion. The military situation was bad and might grow worse.

From the Mediterranean came news that increased his anxiety. Enemy convoys were reaching Tripoli. The latest British convoy had failed to get through to Malta with much-needed supplies and reinforcements. There was no end in sight to the cataract of defeat in the Far East.

And if, in contrast, the Russian scene was sunnier, for the moment, the consolation which this afforded had a nuance of bitterness made almost sharper by the pointed way in which the Russians refrained from reproaching their ally with his failure.

Churchill's Government had been newly reformed and was still untested. He was distrusted by his own party. He had corralled one potential rival, Cripps, but this stroke might have its disadvantages. On that very day, Mr. Alexander Sloan was crowing in the House of Commons over "Churchill's blunder". Cripps, in office, would soon "debunk the amazing theory that the Prime Minister is indispensable". Although Churchill drew comfort from Cripps's powerful and lucid mind, he recognized that here might be a formidable competitor.

Another potential rival, the man who sat with him at the dinner table, was at large. Churchill knew that his friend was loyal—and knew also that personal loyalty could not be the only strand of motive in public affairs.

Two pairs of eyes—the transparent blue, the brooding grey—surveyed one another over the dining-table. The two adventurers, the one from a palace, the other from a manse, so disparate in gifts, so well matched in talent. The aristocrat spoke with the enticing candour which was one of his most attractive resources:

"You told Harold Macmillan 'It is either the Premiership or nothing now' . . . You will be Prime Minister. Nothing can stop it. Events will make you Prime Minister . . . Many of the Ministers will refuse to serve under you."*

He was thinking, perhaps, of Bevin and Cripps, among others.

"But," he went on, "I, Churchill, will be willing to serve you!"[3]

* Mr. Macmillan does not remember the remark. He may have regarded it as jocular.

When every allowance is made for the special political tensions of the hour and the relaxed mood of a dinner-table conversation, it was a remarkable declaration, betraying a momentary invasion of weariness, a recognition that, in the conditions of February 1942, power was indeed a precarious possession.

Churchill went on to shake his head in disapproval over Beaverbrook's lack of wisdom in the manœuvres that had preceded his resignation.

"You made a bad job over the Production Ministry," he said. "If you had lain low for a month, you would have got all you wanted."

But what was it that Beaverbrook wanted just then? To leave the Government, to put aside all the cares of a Minister, above all the cares that he must share with others? That certainly. Had he not sent, over the months, in all thirteen, maybe even fifteen, letters of resignation to the Prime Minister (the tally differed at Number 10 and in Beaverbrook's private office, probably owing to the writer's habit of dashing off a letter of farewell in the car driving home late at night and then withdrawing it verbally next morning); and now the last one had been reluctantly accepted.

The bond of friendship between the two men remained firm, as those who best knew them had predicted it would. A bond made out of profound mutual respect for one another's unusual qualities, plus, on Beaverbrook's side, an acknowledgment, reluctant but whole-hearted, that Churchill was a great man in some way that he was not. Against this admission he might rebel at times—was he not, after all, a more *ingenious* man than Winston?—but it persisted. Even so, it was a salute given by equal to equal. Sir Robert Bruce Lockhart observed that ministers were in the habit of saying, "I am the only man in the Government, apart from Max, who is not afraid of

Winston". From this he drew the logical deduction.

Did Beaverbrook look beyond the resignation, that delusive act of self-liberation? Voices were whispering in London—and uttering more loudly in New York—that he was preparing to become Prime Minister. Some of his most trusted advisers had told him that he would be better out of the Government, free from taint of the disasters that were to come, identified in the mind of the people only with one strenuous and victorious episode, the Battle of Britain. If he may have lent himself at times to these counsels it would be, after all, no more than human.

He was more attentive to more cautious advisers who said, "You are to the public an executant, an energizer. You have not the solemn qualities which the British are accustomed to look for in their statesmen. If you leave the Government—as you are bent on doing—you will begin to fade from men's minds. You—you of all men!—underrate the war-time power of the Government propaganda monopoly to focus the limelight on the men who are still on active duty." Beaverbrook had rejected this advice that he should remain in the Ministry, which does not mean he was influenced to resign by the opposite advice.

What he felt, above all, was that he was being hemmed in as a minister by hostile forces, that he had made enemies (above all, Bevin and Cripps) who meant to bring him down, and that he was, as he put it, "next for the firing squad". This melodramatic view of the situation was, almost certainly, exaggerated. But it was dominant in the imagination of a sensitive and wary man whose nerves were, at that time, stretched to breaking-point.

He resented his own inability to overcome Bevin in the trial of strength, and replace him by a new Minister of Labour—say, Sir Walter Citrine. With Citrine he felt that he could work amicably. The only trouble was that

Citrine would certainly not have accepted the post were it ever offered to him. In fact, it was not. Unreasonable as it might be, Beaverbrook was hurt when Churchill did not prefer him to Bevin at the risk of destroying his Government.

If he appeared at times to fall in with the advice of counsellors at his dinner-table, who urged him to resign so that Britain might have a Prime Minister in reserve, it is probable that he did so merely to rationalize a decision that, in truth, had its origin in temperament and emotions.

What is certain is that he did not at any time set himself up as a pretender to Churchill's throne. He had among his associates men who were actively hostile to the Prime Minister. He may in unguarded moments have measured his talents against Churchill's and decided they were not so incommensurate. There was no harm in pursuing the thread of such idle thoughts. "After all, Pitt said it." But—take the field against his old friend, play Lloyd George to Churchill's Asquith?—Never! This is not a matter of opinion. One day, at this time, Aneurin Bevan called on Beaverbrook at his country home, Cherkley, and asked him to assume the leadership of a movement to bring Churchill down. Beaverbrook listened intently. His answer was "No". The interview came to an unfriendly conclusion.

Churchill was the last man in the world to underrate the political dangers he was in. He acted in the crisis with the same readiness to take defensive precautions as he had shown when he sent Lord Halifax to Washington and Sir Samuel Hoare to Madrid, and when, on three separate occasions in 1940, he had used Beaverbrook as his emissary to draw Lloyd George, the enigmatic hermit of Churt, into the Government. The thrice-repeated mission had failed—although on one occasion it came within an ace of success, Lloyd George being saved from enticement

only by a timely reminder that he had an appointment at
the Belgian Embassy—and now the envoy himself had
become a danger in Churchill's eyes.

Almost a month earlier, Hannen Swaffer had reported
that he had heard rumours, in which he put little credence,
of a plot to make Beaverbrook Prime Minister "with the
backing of big business interests".[4] There was no such
plot but, now that Beaverbrook was free from ministerial
responsibility, stories of that kind were likely to grow, disturbing the political air. So on the day after the dinner-
table conversation, the Prime Minister asked Averell
Harriman to call on Beaverbrook and tell him that he
*must* go to the United States. Harriman did so but was
given no certain answer. At this time, Beaverbrook was torn
between the temptation to escape for a little to the more
pleasant conditions in which he could live in America
and the wish to be in England at a time of suppressed
crisis.

Were he to travel he could make the journey with dignity, the Prime Minister having found him a task to per-
form. He was to persuade Roosevelt, if he could, to allow
Russia to keep the Baltic States after the war. But
Beaverbrook hesitated long before he reached a decision.
Tugging at his mind was the fear that he might be leaving
the political theatre in Britain on the eve of a big scene.
And how he loved the big scenes of politics, whether he
watched them from one of the boxes or took part in them
on the stage!

Already, he felt he had made a tactical blunder in allowing Churchill to account for his resignation by his ill-
health. A sick man is not promoted. And, once he was
safely on the other side of the ocean, be sure (he complained to Liddell Hart) that the Prime Minister would
find fresh excuses to keep him there.[5] Such, in the event,
proved to be far from the case.

Some of this ill-humour spilled over when he came up from the country on 10 March to dine with the Prime Minister. Towards the end of what may have been a depressing meal, Churchill said, not without pathos: "Laugh at my jokes as you used to do, even if they are not very funny." He urged Beaverbrook afresh to go to Washington to discuss the Russian question and then go on as envoy to Moscow "for the German spring offensive", doing everything possible to keep the Russians in the war. Beaverbrook looked on this project without enthusiasm, although he himself had proposed it in the autumn.

Meanwhile, the new epoch of austerity in Britain was welcomed with varying degrees of enthusiasm by the people. For example, the *New Statesman* hoped that economy measures would strike still harder against the rich but, on the other hand, "it is necessary to curb the public zeal of non-smokers and teetotallers for depriving their fellow-citizens of what they regard as noxious drugs".[6]

All in all, there was a disappointing absence of "that uplifting of the spirit which leadership in the grand manner can communicate",[7] and Sir William Beveridge, rather plaintively, asked for "a war of all the people in the spirit of Cromwell's army". It seemed that the presence of Sir Stafford Cripps on the Treasury Bench had not in itself been enough to kindle the sacrificial fire in the people. What is wanted, said *The Economist*, is a spokesman, a Prophet, "to turn his thunders against frustrating futilities".[8]

In conformity with the sterner impulse which Cripps had inaugurated, the nation bore with resignation the news that came with the cold March winds: women's fashions would be simpler, without embroidery, boxing and horse-racing would be restricted, and soon the white loaf would vanish from the bakers' shops.

In the meantime, Lord Beaverbrook found fresh grounds of discontent with his lot. Hore-Belisha, to whom he had confided the secret of his American mission, asked a question in the House of Commons which not only betrayed his knowledge, but had a sting in its tail: he asked for assurances that Lord Beaverbrook's powers would not detract from those of Lord Halifax, the British Ambassador.

But, step by step and with ever-growing irritation, Beaverbrook was being driven to the seaplane at Poole which would take him to Foynes and to Washington. There were one or two last-minute flurries. Attlee, in announcing Lord Beaverbrook's mission in the House of Commons, used a formula which included the words "under Mr. Lyttelton's direction". This was thought to be disparaging, as well as inaccurate. Frantic scenes followed in the suite in the Savoy Hotel which Beaverbrook occupied. A rebellious cry pursued Brendan Bracken (later Lord Bracken) down the corridor: "I won't go. I won't go." But the morning of departure came.

At the last minute, as Beaverbrook, his cases packed, his mind reconciled to the inevitable, was about to go down to his car, Commander Thompson, the Prime Minister's naval aide-de-camp, arrived bearing a letter from Cardinal Hinsley. In this missive the head of the Roman Catholic Church in England set forth with reason and emphasis the antagonism he and his communion felt to the purpose of Beaverbrook's mission. This last warning did not, however, have the power to deter Beaverbrook from the course to which he had condemned himself.

He made the journey through a southern English countryside alive with healthy, tough-looking soldiers, while tanks, guns and all the apparatus of war rumbled or roared between its hedgerows. So to the harbour in Dorset where the seaplane was waiting. But alas, a new disappointment befell at this point. The seaplane had not been earmarked for his private use but was crowded with other passengers. It was a final sting of irritation to the reluctant traveller.

Beaverbrook did not go unremarked. It was said in London at the time: "He is going to the United States to be another thorn in the crown of Lord Halifax." Nor did he go unlamented. In the House of Commons, Mr. Garfield Weston, a rich fellow-Canadian, Conservative M.P. for Macclesfield, complained: "We are told Lord Beaverbrook, one of the outstanding geniuses thrown up by this war, has gone, with hardly a word of regret, because he has asthma. But he has had asthma for twenty years. . . ."

He had left behind a Prime Minister, who, as Lloyd George was saying, almost at that moment, was "childlike, unsure of himself, wanting someone to lean on—and not unwilling that Cripps should take some of the blame". In his Cabinet Churchill found little comfort.[9] A fortnight after Beaverbrook's departure, Ernest Bevin and A. V. Alexander reported to their colleagues that Labour was discontented with the way the war was going. What a pity it was that the public could not be given a full explanation! But had such an explanation been possible, it would hardly have swept away the clouds of woe.

A Japanese fleet of four fast battleships and five aircraft-carriers, with attendant cruisers and destroyers, had entered the Indian Ocean. They had pounced on the Andaman Islands and were threatening Ceylon. Against them, Admiral Somerville mustered, at Addu Atoll, five old battleships—four of them slow—two carriers and a couple of cruisers. Admiral Sir Geoffrey Layton, Commander-in-Chief of the Ceylon station, had snatched two squadrons of Hurricanes on their way to Java, warned by a last signal from a doomed Catalina that the Japanese were approaching.

Layton made his thirty-six Hurricanes ready for battle. When the attack came on Easter morning (5 April) these fighters shot down twenty-one of a force of eighty Japanese bombers. Half the fighters were lost, a British merchant cruiser and a destroyer were sunk, but Ceylon was for the moment saved and Admiral Somerville's ancient warships were able to withdraw 2,000 miles westwards to Africa and safety.

The air battles over Ceylon on that day and the day following marked, as it proved, a turning point in the naval war in the Indian Ocean. But this was not yet realized by the anxious men at Churchill's Cabinet table. "Cairo was none too safe, Persia was threatened . . . India's eastern flank was threatened, vital communications through the Indian Ocean might be cut at any moment, and Australia and New Zealand even open to attack."[10] Truly the prospect was as bleak as it was vast, more precarious, so thought Sir Alan Brooke, Chief of the Imperial General Staff, than at any hour in the history of the British Empire. Saved once by a miracle at Dunkirk, was it reasonable to expect a second intervention by Providence?

Three days after the Colombo air battle, while everything still hung in the balance, Harry Hopkins and General George Marshall stepped from their aeroplane at Hendon. They were the bearers of momentous proposals from President Roosevelt.

# CHAPTER X

# *Stitching is not strategy*

*There is only one test for a class's fitness to rule—its ability to wage war.*
—André Malraux, 1948, reported by Janet Flanner
in the *Paris Journal*, p. 84

IN THE MIDDLE OF APRIL 1942 there broke out what Aneurin Bevan's *Tribune* optimistically described as "the palace revolt against Churchill". In this movement it discerned newspapers as important as *The Times*, the *Sunday Times* and *The Observer*; statesmen as respectable as Lords Salisbury, Swinton and Hankey. There was also Sir Edward Grigg, who it could be said, first raised the rebel standard with an article in *The Times*. In this he said that the existing organization of Britain's grand strategy was mistaken and harmful.

There was a Defence Committee over which Mr. Churchill presided as Minister of Defence. There ought, instead, to be a Great General Staff who would, in fact, be composed of the professional heads of the three services, with a professional chairman whose duty it would be to sift out the various strategic ideas of the services, test them by realistic criteria and, having selected, trimmed and refined these notions, present the ensuing product to the final judgment of the Prime Minister and the War Cabinet. The chairman himself would have no executive powers. He would merely serve as a conduit and filter.

The conception launched by Grigg was taken up by Lord Hankey, a veteran with all the authority of an ex-Minister and ex-Secretary of the Cabinet, who thought of Churchill as a "rogue elephant" who, unlike the rogue elephant of the previous war, Lloyd George, lacked "two wise old elephants" like Milner and Smuts to guide him. Hankey argued that it was not enough to bundle together the ideas of the three services. He reminded the House of Lords of Lloyd George's dictum: "Stitching is not strategy."

Hearing of Hankey's criticism, Beaverbrook, by this time in the United States, sent Roosevelt a caustic note: "Hankey drew a bonus of £25,000 from public moneys for being good at defending Lloyd George a quarter of a century ago. He also pulled down a peerage and got a place in the Chamberlain Government. He knows a great deal and says it at great length."[1]

*The Spectator* (3 April) uncovered a little further the thinking that lay behind the "palace revolt". Running the war, it said, ought to be the responsibility of the Cabinet as a whole. This would create "a larger cadre of potential Prime Ministers" and, in a long war, with the Prime Minister running great risks, it was important to have trained replacements. The editor concluded with a piece of reasoning that was puzzling rather than convincing: "The more the indispensability of Mr. Churchill impresses itself, the more essential does it appear that there should be someone to replace him in case of need."

Ignoring any criticism that might be offered them, the "rebels" kept up their outcry for "one with a forceful mind to submit plans", "one full-time man at the brain centre". *The Economist*, more cautiously, joined the advocates of unity of command by means of "a Great Captain and Great General Staff". The *New Statesman*, in which Mr. Kingsley Martin was, about that time, calling the people to arms,[2] registered the opinion that Grigg had won "the most powerful support".

This was also the opinion of Lord Beaverbrook, who gave President Roosevelt his own sprightly version of these events in a summary of the British press which he sent the President from Miami Beach, where he was staying. He reported "a new attack" on Churchill's position as Defence Minister, launched by Grigg ("connected with the Cliveden school of politics") and continued by Hankey, whom Churchill had sacked in February. "Hankey replied with a very bitter letter, denouncing in retrospect Churchill's war strategy. . . . A third protagonist is Lord Salisbury . . . a dangerous foe."[3]

But was the Grigg Plan a sound one? Would the overall strategic genius (Wavell? Alexander? Lord Chatfield, a name mentioned by *The Times*?) really produce the smoother flow of better operational thinking that was hoped for? Or would he be simply an additional storey in the existing pyramid of war direction which *The Spectator* described with no excessive enthusiasm ("an imposing diagram")? If the ideas he fathered were bad, would the War Cabinet limit itself to rejecting them without putting forward proposals for revision? If, on the other hand, they were good, would he be content to remain in a non-executive role?

One man must have seen the origins and drift of the Plan with extreme clarity: Churchill. To him this was simply a new manifestation of the criticism of his conduct of the war which had been rumbling on now for six months. It was more sophisticated than most of its predecessors. It came from well-informed professionals. Being a connoisseur of irony, the Prime Minister would not fail to relish the exquisite touch where *The Spectator* put forward his "indispensability" as an argument for training his "replacement".

Revolt was not, however, confined to "the palace". It was apparent from various symptoms that a wind of social unrest was rising after the long calm imposed by the war and that, under its force, the ship of inter-party unity was springing a leak.

For example, in the *Daily Mirror*, "Cassandra" (the late Sir William Connor), a brilliant and caustic columnist, launched an attack on the leadership of the Army: "At the top you have the military aristocracy of the Guards, with a mentality not very foreign to that of Potsdam. In the centre, you have a second-class snobocracy." These were opinions unlikely to be pleasing to Churchill, who long since suspected the *Daily Mirror* of something akin to treason and who regarded any criticism of the military hierarchy as tantamount to undermining the morale of the army. As Brendan Bracken said, "Winston is still a 4th Hussar."

Although "Cassandra" was attacking on a narrow front, his words breathed a novel and alarming disrespect. There were other signs that the freeze in British politics was not likely to last. In three by-elections, Conservative seats were lost to Independent candidates.

At Grantham in Lincolnshire, Denis Kendall, a "ginger candidate", defeated Air-Chief-Marshal Sir Arthur Longmore by 367 votes. Mr. Kendall, a manufacturer of guns, declared: "Churchill says he doesn't want me. But he has me. I am the youngest member of the Gun Board." The local Conservatives were tactless enough to complain that the election was "not cricket", while local Labour Party members, showing a tendency to give support to Kendall, himself a member of the party, were warned by an official sent to the spot that their activities were causing embarrassment in Transport House.

The contest was fought with the full austerity of wartime electioneering—no election favours; one election address to each household; limited supplies of petrol to candidates; meetings restricted so as to save light and heat. Kendall's victory, on a simple policy which Lord Beaverbrook might have phrased, "Away with all bottlenecks, and hang politics", was regarded by the Government as a shock, salutary rather than damaging.

A month after the Grantham by-election two more seats were snatched by Independents. On the last day of April, Mr. W. J. Brown, leader of the Civil Service Association, won Rugby by 679 votes; and Mr. G. L. Reakes took Wallasey by 6,012. Conforming to the pious formula of the time, Reakes said that his win was a victory for Churchill; Brown ascribed his to popular resentment at the domination of the party machines. Somewhat like Kendall at Grantham, he had fought on the slogan, "Total Efficiency for Total War"; as his campaign progressed, he laid growing emphasis on the need for a "Second Front".

The double election blow caused some commotion in Parliament; it was "unpleasant and disturbing news to the Government"[4]; while the *Evening Standard* drew the deduction that party leaders would be well advised to drop the political truce "like a hot brick", an opinion which puzzled A. J. Cummings but was in close conformity with the general views of the Beaverbrook press at the time— party leaders, members of the same administration, espousing the claims of rival candidates; Mr. Churchill, Prime Minister, urging local electors to vote against a Labour candidate recommended by Mr. Attlee, Deputy Prime Minister; party machines engaged in local battles up and down the country—were the "hot brick" dropped a national conflagration might follow, with unpredictable consequences! The frightening notion may not have been seriously put forward by its champions; it was not seriously considered by anyone else.

*Tribune* (8 May) surveyed the by-election scene with

unconcealed satisfaction: "The presence in Parliament of a number of Members free from coercion by party machines will be the best medicine that Parliament has had for more than a century. Rugby sent W. J. Brown to Westminster in spite of a special curse from the National Council of Labour. Cripps, expelled from the party, is now in the Cabinet." The victor of Wallasey was a supporter of the Popular Front, an institution hated by all obedient Labour members but dear to Cripps and Aneurin Bevan.

It seemed that, in Cripps, the twin strands of social discontent and annoyance with military failure might be entwined. He visited India at this time (22 March to 12 April) on a mission the purpose of which was to win the co-operation of the Indian nationalists in the war by an offer of partial self-government, with an option of independence after the war was over. But—Singapore had fallen, Burma was overrun by the Japanese, Britain's prestige in the East had sunk low. Gandhi described the offers Cripps brought as "post-dated cheques upon a bankrupt Empire". The hopes with which Cripps set out foundered.

Nevertheless, the idealism he embodied retained its power, suggesting to Eve Curie that she "was witnessing the awakening of a new spirit in England, bold, generous". When he broadcast on the lack of urgency in Britain's war he had almost as big an audience as Churchill himself.

The Gallup Poll brought its testimony to support the belief that a momentous change in popular feeling had occurred. Every month the Poll asked the question "After Churchill, who do you think should be Prime Minister?" In November 1941, thirty-eight per cent of those with definite opinions answered, Eden; Beaverbrook came second with eleven per cent. In April 1942, Eden had thirty-seven per cent of the preferences, Beaverbrook's share

had fallen to two (either because of his disappearance
from the ministerial firmament or because the reports of
his ill-health had been taken at their face value), but
Cripps had appeared, as it were from nowhere, to claim
thirty-four per cent.

While the *New Statesman* (2 May) brooded on "The
Problem of Mr. Churchill", *Tribune* (1 May) asked bluntly through the voice of "Thomas Rainborough": "Why
Churchill?" The writer, "a publicist with unrivalled knowledge", was Mr. Frank Owen, editor of the *Evening Standard*, whom Aneurin Bevan, following his plan of drawing
into his unrewarding service journalists "with good information and bad consciences", had persuaded to contri-
bute to *Tribune*.

Owen-Rainborough set himself to consider "the great
premiership" with the unfriendly eye of one who thought
that "if Churchill saved Britain in June 1940, Britain also
did a bit towards saving Churchill and his party". He was
unimpressed by the strategic powers of "the modern
Marlborough"[5] who, in Greece, had "thrown away his
country's finest opportunity". If, as Aneurin Bevan said,
building up Churchill's reputation "has gone as far as the
safety of the country warrants", Rainborough had made
a manful start on the work of demolition. This was interrupted, when at the end of March, Owen was called up for
the Army, an event which Lord Beaverbrook greeted in a
light-hearted cable from America: "My boy, my boy, my
pride and joy, where is my boy tonight?" As a serving
soldier, Owen was debarred from delivering speeches urging a Second Front.

As the spring of 1942 warmed into summer, the Prime
Minister was aware of the doubting approval of Parliament and sometimes—when he broadcast to the nation
"over its head"—of its jealousy, He had annoyed the
Left by throwing his mantle over the discredited Right

when he assumed the leadership of the Conservative Party. And the Right would never trust him. The professionals of war, the old hands, generals, admirals, civil servants, found his methods of conducting the struggle impulsive and disorderly, his manners bad and his strategy worse. He could afford to ignore their murmurings. Against him were critics who, short of some unimaginable catastrophe, were unlikely to be cemented together.

The soldiers, suspicious by their upbringing of all politicians, looked with particular distaste on the seething Left which for its part (if Rainborough be excluded) cared nothing for strategy. There was no sign of a common ground of attack, unless perhaps it existed in embryo in the Second Front agitation. Already it might be noticed that a phrase used by Stalin in a message to Churchill would turn up, exactly reproduced, in a *Tribune* article a month or two later. A lively suspicion existed that the Russian Ambassador did not confine his activities to the stricter channels of diplomacy. As the summer passed, with no British action on the Continent, more would be heard of this matter.

In the meantime, Churchill could take comfort from the Gallup Polls which showed that while changes might occur in the relative popularity of the pretenders to his throne, his own leadership remained serenely above every rivalry. At a dark moment in the battle, the British had given their hearts to a great captain; they were not the kind of people to withdraw their loyalty merely because they suspected that he was not an infallible strategist.

Ludwell Denny, the Scripps-Howard news commentator, observed that British voters were defeating Government candidates because they wanted a Second Front. "This demand has a familiar ring to Americans. Only a few days ago they heard it from Lord Beaverbrook" (*Sunday Express*, 3 May, 1942).

The fugitive from Mr. Churchill's Government had not spent his time in idleness. He had flown to Washington where he consulted with the President and Harry Hopkins. Then he retired to a comfortable hotel in the sunshine of Miami Beach.

With rest and the change of scene, Beaverbrook began slowly to recover command of his overwrought nerves, slowly to see things in better perspective. He had, too, an important assignment ahead of him, the delivery of a speech before an audience which, for influence and power, could hardly be surpassed in the United States or anywhere else. He withdrew to Sea Island, Georgia, a secluded seaside colony for weary millionaires, to apply himself in solitude, and with his customary thoroughness and enthusiasm, to the tasks of preparation. It was to be a political speech, a speech in which policy—his policy at least—would be stated and by which policy would be shaped. It was to be a bid for influence over a public which, in effect, was co-extensive with the English-speaking world. Its main theme was to be the Second Front.

No wonder then that all the time he and his secretary worked on the speech beside that glorious beach in Georgia, Beaverbrook was gripped by the excited glee of a naughty schoolboy, alternately exulting in his own daring and apprehensive of future chastisement.

For he knew that on this matter of the Second Front there was a complete divergence of opinion between himself and Winston Churchill. And he was in the United States, in however vague a capacity, as an envoy of the British Government. He knew that what he was about to say could enrage the Prime Minister. He was alarmed at the probable consequences. Yet he knew that he would say it.

When the speech was completed and his thoughts were reduced to the customary handful of notes, he set off to New York, travelling by way of Washington, where Lord Halifax found him "obsessed with English politics" (Halifax's Diary, 2 April, 1942). But his main business in Washington was not with the British Ambassador but with the President and Harry Hopkins.

On 23 April, he was due to speak in the Waldorf Astoria Hotel in New York to 1,100 members and guests of the Bureau of Advertising of the American Newspaper Publishers' Association, including distinguished figures like Admiral King, Commander-in-Chief of the U.S. Navy, Major-General McNarney, Deputy Chief of Staff of the U.S. Army, and Francis B. Sayre, High Commissioner to the Philippines. Unseen, beyond, there would be a vast radio audience.

Ten, twenty times that day Beaverbrook rehearsed the speech in his suite at the Waldorf Towers. He was even muttering its phrases as he went down in the lift. It was important that he should be word-perfect.

The climax of the speech and of the evening came when he urged that Britain should adopt the policy of Stalin, "a master of tactics", and set up, somewhere along the 2,000 miles of coastline now held by the Germans, a Second Front.

Coming from the lips of one who had left the British administration two months earlier, this unequivocal demand was of the liveliest interest to those who heard it. Here was the British ex-Minister of Supply advocating on a foreign soil a strategy which the Russians and the Communists were known to want and for which Mr. Churchill had, so far, shown no signs of enthusiasm.

Was there, in Lord Beaverbrook's strident and elliptic declamation, so much better fitted to communicate a sense of urgency than to convey an argument, some relic of a dispute with the Prime Minister about high policy? *Was this why Lord Beaverbrook had quit?*

The trained minds assembled in the banqueting room of the Waldorf Astoria must have pondered the question.

"Strike out to help Russia. Strike out violently. Strike even recklessly." Who was standing in the way of such daring? Some unnamed persons lurking in the British Government? "Public men should be subjected to criticism," Beaverbrook insisted.

But not, it seemed, "our own great leader, Mr. Churchill" to whom the orator devoted the last 300 words of his address, praising the Prime Minister in unmeasured terms and begging his listeners to help him to kill "the bad rumour" that Churchill would fall before the summer was out. "Such a disaster we cannot contemplate in Great Britain. We are grateful to him for all that he has done in the past. And, of course, we can pay him off in coins of gratitude. But in truth we are not capable of such folly. For it is his service in days to come that we count on."

The final effect of the remarkable speech, due in a few days' time to be distributed in Britain by the *Daily Express* as a pamphlet, was equivocal. The voices prophesying Churchill's downfall had been denounced; and their message had been repeated so that it could be denied. The panegyric of the British Prime Minister was associated with the acknowledgment that some of the ministers he tolerated might deserve condemnation. Nor was this all. Responsibility for the defeat in Greece a year before was firmly placed on Churchill who ("I do not hesitate to tell you") had ordered that expedition in full knowledge of the sacrifices it would entail.

It was almost as if the supreme moral qualities of the Prime Minister were being extolled, nearly to excess, by one who hinted at certain weaknesses of judgment in the hero. If that were a fair interpretation of the speech nobody could deny that the criticisms came from a loyal friend, a well-instructed source, a proven executive. But would he take part in dealing with the crises that lay ahead? This question was implied by his speech and was left unanswered.

On both shores of the Atlantic the after-dinner oratory at the Waldorf Astoria caused perturbation. The *New York Times* reported "mixed" reactions from London, where some people believed it to presage Beaverbrook's early return to politics—and opposition politics at that. Others in Britain, of his way of thinking, adopted the slogan "Victory in 1942".

On the whole, American military opinion was believed to be more favourable than British;[6] Beaverbrook had expressed a universal wish[7]—but his plea for reckless attack was deprecated by the experts.[8] The *New York Times*[9]— the editor of which, Mr. Arthur Sulzberger, had heard the speech with deep emotion, declared that "on both sides of the Atlantic, the belief is strong that we cannot afford to waste the present opportunity. The hour for attack lies near at hand."

In London the *Sunday Times* thought the speech unfortunate and *The Economist*[10] asked, with some severity, if Lord Beaverbrook was prepared to state openly that the ships, weapons and aircraft for an expeditionary force were ready and that "only intransigence or worse" held the invasion back.

"It is a gross disservice to the high spirit of the people to suggest . . . that they are being misled, held back, and betrayed at the peak of their resolution—just as it would be a betrayal . . . for the Government to prepare a larger and more disastrous Crete or Gallipoli under polemical pressure."

The leader-writer of the *Daily Herald*,[11] who often echoed the opinions of Ernest Bevin, said that Beaverbrook appeared to be declaring himself "dissatisfied with the strategic policy of the Cabinet to which he so lately belonged" and found it hard to reconcile the views of speakers who, "in one and the same speech, fulsomely praise the Prime Minister and criticize his Government's policy".

Was the praise of Churchill the man as sincere as the criticism of his Government? The question troubled many observers who were puzzled rather than convinced by the vehemence of Lord Beaverbrook's championship of his friend. The *Sunday Times* rebuked Lord Beaverbrook for stamping on a "non-existent" rumour that Churchill would fall before the summer is out. And A. J. Cummings, always quick to come to the aid of his friend Beaverbrook, rebuked the *Sunday Times*: "Newspapermen on both sides of the Atlantic knew all about the rumour and he did well to end it."[12]

The man most interested of all had his own individual comment to make. Churchill, talking to a group of American journalists and broadcasters, was asked what he thought of Lord Beaverbrook's speech. "A very fine speech," he replied. But what did he think of the references to the Second Front? The Prime Minister savoured his answer roguishly before uttering it. "I would rather have him preaching the Second Front than a negotiated peace, wouldn't you?" he said.

The humour was not lost on his hearers, most of whom remembered the episode in the House of Commons which, at the time, had been so irritating to Mr. Churchill, Mr. McGovern and Lord Beaverbrook.

In fact Beaverbrook, who, before delivering his speech, had discussed it at length with the President and Harry Hopkins, had not "cleared" it with the Prime Minister.[13] Churchill had read newspaper accounts of the speech with dismay.

A few hours before Lord Beaverbrook rose to speak in New York, the Prime Minister had sat down in the House of Commons at the conclusion of one of the frankest and most melancholy speeches ever delivered in a secret session of Parliament. Its theme was the fall of Singapore, a loss so much more bitter and crushing than anything that had been foreseen that it could neither be minimized nor excused. "The violence, fury, skill and might of Japan has far exceeded anything that we had been led to expect." After so grievous an avowal of faulty prescience, ill-conceived dispositions and scrimped resources, the House of Commons was not likely to be in the mood to favour new military adventures. But what was said behind locked doors in Westminster would not be heard outside. Beaverbrook had spoken to a wider public, in two continents. And he had sounded the charge.

Churchill recognized that his friend had given a new dignity and importance to what had been little more than a slogan chalked on the walls by obedient members of the Communist Party. A bold attempt was being made to influence Britain's strategy by popular agitation. The military hierarchy might be outraged, the Prime Minister might deplore, but the Second Front could not easily be swept under the carpet, nor left to the secret and undisturbed deliberations of staff officers.

By transatlantic telephone, Churchill suggested to Beaverbrook that he should return home. The summons was obeyed, although Beaverbrook took the precaution of bringing with him a recording of the Waldorf Astoria speech so that the Prime Minister could hear it in full and judge it fairly. Before leaving, he had a final talk with Lord Halifax, with whom he had enjoyed a long acquaintanceship which had not warmed into friendship. Soon after Beaverbrook found himself a member of Churchill's government in 1940, he was a neighbour of Halifax's, at dinner. In his expansive way, Beaverbrook said that, since becoming Minister of Aircraft Production, he had given up all financial ties with his newspapers. Halifax said, "But, Max, won't you find it rather difficult to rub along on a Minister's salary?"

Beaverbrook answered, "But, Edward, you forget I have the royalties on 'Guilty Men'."

In this once famous war-time pamphlet, "appeasers" like Halifax had been severely handled. "Guilty Men" was the joint work of Michael Foot, Peter Howard and Frank Owen, three of Beaverbrook's employees. Some of the lurid light of their exploit was unfairly reflected on Beaverbrook.

Halifax now found Beaverbrook "in a rather difficult mood" and quite uncertain what he should do when he returned to London. He believed that the Government's position was weak, and that he himself would have a considerable following. This was, at any rate, the impression formed by Halifax, who sent the Prime Minister a telegram telling him what he thought Beaverbrook meant to do.

One of the things Beaverbrook did after his return to Britain was to set up an organization called the Centre of Public Opinion, an agency of propaganda supported by the Express newspapers. Mr. John Gordon, editor of the *Sunday Express*, a natural and forceful agitator, presided over the inaugural meeting of the Centre, held at the London Hippodrome in Leicester Square on Sunday afternoon, 24 May. The purpose of the meeting was explicitly stated in the publicity material which preceded it. "Subject: The Second Front, the most important issue of the day. . . . There will be complete liberty of speech, subject only to the needs of security. Admission will be free by ticket only." The audience of 1,400 was outnumbered by those whose applications for tickets had been refused.

While they waited for the speeches, the lucky 1,400 sang patriotic songs.

This and later demonstrations organized by the Centre met a real need in war-time Britain, the lack of entertainment if not of instruction. The people were starved of opportunities to take part in the discussion of public questions. In normal times, it is hard to realize how black-out, petrol-rationing and similar oppressions had driven each British household in on itself, to become the mute, anxious audience of the nine o'clock news of the B.B.C. Naturally, the meetings of the Centre were seized on with special enthusiasm by the Communists, who recognized in them a heaven-sent opportunity for Second Front propaganda. Soon the sponsors of the Centre became anxious to prevent "an organization which holds meetings about which there is much speculation"[14] from becoming a Communist monopoly, to the embarrassment of the Government and Lord Beaverbrook.

As Beaverbrook was well aware when he spoke in New York, General George Marshall and Mr. Harry Hopkins had arrived in London on 8 April bringing to Churchill a memorandum[15] by President Roosevelt in which he proposed an invasion of Western Europe by forty-eight British and American divisions supported by 5,000 combat aircraft. As this could not be mounted before 1 April, 1943, a plan should be prepared for a smaller emergency operation to take advantage of a sudden German disintegration or to avert an imminent Russian collapse. On the evening of 14 April, a joint Anglo-American conference met at Number 10 Downing Street to discuss these grave matters.

There was—or there appeared to be—unanimity in favour of a frontal assault on the enemy in 1943 but many doubts about General Marshall's idea that the Cherbourg peninsula might be seized by a (mainly British) attack in the autumn of 1942. Churchill vastly preferred a descent on French North-West Africa and, as an alternative or possibly as an addition, he hankered after an invasion of Northern Norway. The operation in North Africa might, he thought, usefully fill the gap in time until Europe could be invaded in 1943. The possibility that the descent on North Africa might, in fact, postpone the main invasion of Europe was something that the strategists in Downing Street do not seem to have contemplated. But was there a real meeting of minds between the Americans and the British?

It had been an odd encounter in some respects, with the Americans, whose main interest was in the war in the Far East, pressing for action in Europe, while the British, bent on destroying Hitler, pointed to the mounting danger to India as a reason for going slow in the West. The Prime Minister did not disclose to his allies the full extent of his doubts about the President's "momentous proposal" for a large-scale invasion of Europe before April 1943. As he said later, "I had to work by influence and by diplomacy to secure agreed and harmonious action."[16] He kept his counsel and relied on time and close study by professional soldiers to do half the work of dissuasion for him. Hopkins was therefore unaware of the range and obstinacy of Churchill's real strategic intentions when he returned to Washington and consulted with Beaverbrook a few days before the latter rose to speak in the Waldorf Astoria banqueting-room.

Among responsible statesmen outside the Soviet Union these two men were the most outspoken protagonists of a Second Front strategy. The project already had the seal of "H.H." on it,[17] a talisman only second in magic and power to the initials "F.D.R." at the time when Beaverbrook's "Strike out to help Russia—even recklessly" startled the massed diners in New York. But it seemed that, even without such public advocacy, the Second Front case had won. General Marshall was reported to have returned from London convinced that the time for action was near. Roosevelt was said to agree. "The hour for attack lies near at hand," concluded the *New York Times.*[18]

## CHAPTER XI

# A Government of youth

*The people's prayer, the glad diviner's theme,*
*The young men's vision and the old men's dream.*
John Dryden

As SPRING ADVANCED, two facts became clear: Churchill's hold on the heart of the nation was as strong as
ever, and the professional objections to his manner of
conducting the war simmered on, breaking out here and
there in criticisms that were obviously well-informed. It
was argued, for instance, by one journal[1] that the Prime
Minister influenced the military judgment of the Chiefs
of Staff too early in the formulation of policy.

Through General Ismay, who knew his mind on strategic matters better than anyone else (said the newspaper),
his opinions were heard in the Chiefs of Staff Committee.
When the findings of this committee were passed up to the
Defence Committee, who was in the chair but Mr. Churchill! The next stage was the War Cabinet itself, with
whom lay the power of final ratification. And there in the
chair sat the Prime Minister.

"Whereas the War Cabinet should have before it a
strictly scientific appreciation on which to found its final
judgment, it may on crucial occasions actually have a brief
already coloured by ministerial influence at too early a
stage." The Prime Minister was impatient, apt to pursue
a "magnificently nonsensical" policy of attacking the

enemy wherever he might be found, fascinated by War
Rooms and over-inclined to play Marlborough in
dramatic conferences staged at fantastic hours of the
night. This description was, of course, a compendious
statement of what might be called the general's case
against the "dominant but unlucky" man who was their
master. It was a most closely reasoned and most damaging attack upon the system by which the war was being
conducted. It described a process by which an error was
more likely to be perpetuated than eliminated.

But the British public was not likely to frown upon
Churchill because he worked the generals unreasonably
hard. It seemed that the portrait of him conjured up by
his critics, a man bubbling with ideas, energy and all un-
reasonableness, was by no means distasteful to the citi-
zens. If he had an excessive propensity to attack, it was a
weakness which the people shared. As for the attempt to
fasten on him the adjective "unlucky", the nation remembered that Churchill had taken over responsibility for the
war at the moment when Britain's fortunes were at the
lowest they had ever known. Churchill, it was clear,
shrank from a second direct confrontation in Europe with
the main force of the German Army. He sought devious
approaches, flanking movements, limited operations. In
this, he was not simply a romantic delighting in the
beauty of a small effort which produces a surprisingly
large effect. He was also the provident steward of his
nation's human stock, depleted by the four years' car-
nage on the Western Front. "It's no use," said Lord
Cherwell to General Marshall, who was stating the case to
Churchill for an immediate invasion of France. "You are
arguing against the casualties on the Somme."[2] Churchill's caution, as well as his daring, could win an echo in
the British heart.

Any doubts the Prime Minister may have felt about the

place he held in Britain's heart must have been completely dissipated by a visit he paid to Leeds at this time. He told a crowd of 25,000 outside Leeds Town Hall: "None of us is weary of the struggle, none of us is asking for any favours." The crowd had not assembled by magic. Early that morning, the Leeds police had left leaflets announcing the meeting at houses in the town. Still, it was a warming and stirring occasion which one of his companions compared to "a triumphal procession".

Churchill returned to London spiritually refreshed by the experience, convinced that his personal standing in the country was as high as ever and that his Government was perceptibly stronger than it had been a month earlier. Sir Stafford Cripps might be failing to command the House of Commons. In a by-election at Chichester an independent candidate might score 10,000 votes against the Conservative. These things could be seen in proportion. As for the snarls in the newspapers against his management of the war, it was plain that they awoke no echoes outside London and few echoes outside Whitehall.

More important by far were the differences about basic strategic problems which had sprung up between the allies: the Russians in their military extremity pressing for a Second Front, and not caring by what methods they achieved their purpose, nor what the cost might be to Britain; the Americans, more anxious than the British about the gigantic battle on the steppes, which was now breaking out again after the winter lull and was due to take the German Army to the west bank of the Volga and within sight of the Caspian Sea.

Could the Russians stay in the war? The question aroused more perturbation in the White House than at Number 10 Downing Street. Churchill had never really budged from the position which he had stated, with some brutality, to Cripps in October 1941, while the latter was still at Kuibyshev: "They [the Russians] brought their own fate upon themselves when . . . they let Hitler loose on Poland."[3] He felt himself under no moral obligation to Stalin. And, less involved emotionally with the Russians than some others were, he was able to take a cooler view of their chances of survival. Nothing must subtract from the primary claim of the battle in the desert, nothing.

Above all, there must not be a premature landing in Western Europe. Every argument was pressed into service to prevent such a blunder. The American planners were reminded of Britain's sacred duty to defend India against the Japanese and of the danger that the Germans and Japanese might join hands across the world. This, as we know, was the ultimate purpose of Admiral Raeder's "Great Plan". Those two allies were at the moment roughly 3,000 miles apart as the crow flies, with oceans, savage mountain chains, and waterless deserts stretching between them. But in the magic of Churchillian eloquence the distances melted, the oceans shrank, the mountains were made low and listeners were persuaded, while the spell lasted, that the most imminent of military dangers was a vast conjunction of forces which was, in fact, remote and unlikely. The truth, which could not be known in London, was that the Japanese had already given up the idea of pressing further west on the seas.

As a tribute to force of character and consistency of purpose, however, nothing is so remarkable as Churchill's dogged defence of his chosen strategy against his two chief allies, each of whom thought he was not fighting the war hard enough, and against his generals, who thought he was fighting it too hard. Whatever happened, the Prime Minister was determined to keep the conduct of the war firmly and decisively in his own hands.

In the last days of May, London enjoyed a false summer of euphoria. The Russians, it was believed, were delighted with the way Timoshenko's attack on Kharkov was progressing, while, in the Libyan Desert, Rommel's tank offensive—forestalling one by the British Eighth Army—was developing more or less as the British staff had expected; it was about to be repelled. "Well done, Eighth Army," was the signal from Cairo to the desert when the battered German forces shrank back through the minefields. Meanwhile, had not a force of 1,000 British aircraft including some training aircraft, bombed Cologne and left in ruins 600 acres of the city?

The comfort which such events brought to the war-worn British people did not last long.

It was, in truth, ill-founded. At the moment when Whitehall was rejoicing in a supposed Russian victory, Timoshenko, after making two vain appeals to Moscow for permission to withdraw, had accepted total defeat. Three-quarters of the strength—and all the heavy equipment—of the Russian 6th and 9th Armies was left behind on the west bank of the Donetz river. On the Russian southern and south-western front 200 tanks, a mere sprinkling of battle-worn survivors, prepared to meet the impending German summer campaign, which would be armed with almost ten times as powerful a force.

In Libya, disaster trod on the heels of success. In a renewed, concentrated assault, Rommel destroyed the dispersed British armour at "Knightsbridge" on 12 June. In its greatest defeat of the war, the Eighth Army lost 260 "I" tanks. So swiftly had the tables been turned that *The Economist*, which appeared on the following day, was caught remarking that at few times since the war started had the news sounded better.

Gazing with little enthusiasm at the evidence of yet another failure in Africa, the nation suffered an additional

blow: two convoy operations designed to take vital supplies to Malta were defeated. Raeder's "Great Plan" was
brought that much nearer to success. Mercifully, the public knew only in the most general terms of the course of
the wider war waged against allied merchant shipping by
submarine, mine and aircraft and now approaching a
savage climax. The total losses during 1942 were 7,500,000
tons, nearly double those of 1941. To give some measure
of the magnitude of this slaughter, the output of new tonnage from British yards during 1942 was 1,300,000 tons.

Amid such nearer and sobering preoccupations, one
event greater than any of them made an inadequate impact on the public. In the vicinity of Midway Island, in the
central Pacific, an outnumbered fleet of American carriers
routed a Japanese fleet bent on the capture of the island.
Four Japanese carriers were sunk for the loss of one
American. It was six months, to a day, after Pearl
Harbour.

This naval victory was, as it turned out, decisive in the
Pacific War. It meant that the Japanese would not be able
to invade Australia or advance upon the Middle East.
Their belated attempt to clinch the advantage gained at
Pearl Harbour had failed. However, the full fruits of the
American success could not quickly be gathered and,
achieved as it was in the remote expanses of the Pacific, its
consoling message was weakened for the British people.
They were concerned with nearer, smaller and less cheer-
ful matters.

On 26 May, at the end of a visit by Molotov to the West,
an Anglo-Russian Treaty was signed in London, As the
price paid for failing to recognize Russian sovereignty over
the Baltic States—Latvia, Estonia and Lithuania—Britain
conceded a twenty years' mutual security agreement.

Beaverbrook thought that Russia's sovereignty should have been conceded. In fact, his last visit to Washington had ostensibly been concerned with the questions of the Baltic States.

To mark his disapproval of the Treaty, he absented himself from the ceremonial luncheon at the Soviet Embassy. His ostentatious detachment from the Government at this time was remarked, with irritation by Eden, with anxiety by Churchill and with displeasure by Roosevelt and Hopkins, two men whose good opinion Beaverbrook particularly cherished.

Churchill, who could not be completely happy so long as his formidable and restless friend was not welded into the structure of government, considered ways of tempting Beaverbrook back into service. For instance, if Lord Halifax were brought home from the Washington Embassy, who could better take his place than Max, who had the entrée to the White House?

Another perceptive eye was aware of the possibilities latent in Beaverbrook's self-exile from the Government. Lloyd George, who had been in a belligerent and confident mood for some time, now reverted to his original belief in a stalemate end to the struggle. He sent a message to Lord Beaverbrook. It was terse and dramatic in form:

"Say nothing. Then in two months' time let your newspapers start a demand for a Government of Youth. Form it!"

It was, as Lord Beaverbrook thought, strange advice for one old man to give another. It was not advice that he was likely to take. After the enormous attention which had been aroused by his speech in New York, there had been a time when his numerous admiring friends found in him a receptive audience. This mood did not last long. He had the temperament to enjoy applause and the judgment to distrust it.

His admirers were not always so sagacious. Some formed a committee to advance Beaverbrook's political fortunes. One of them paid a fee of 250 guineas to Leadley's, a public relations firm in London, to start a "whispering campaign" in the bars of the West End suggesting that, were anything to happen to Churchill, Beaverbrook would be the natural successor. Wind of this agitation came—as most things did—to the Prime Minister's ears. He mentioned the matter to Beaverbrook, who was deeply embarrassed. After a word from him to his misguided supporter, the whispers in the London bars died away. Meanwhile, in the entourage of Sir Stafford Cripps, it was thought that Beaverbrook calculated Churchill would fall by June and would be succeeded by him.

Yet, with the war going badly and soon to go worse, there was plainly room at Churchill's elbow for a man who united a cold brain and a kindling spirit, for the particular mixture of harshness and subtlety, of the creative and the executive, which gave its unique tang to Beaverbrook's personality. Churchill was more aware of this than anyone else. He missed his friend and he was anxious —not on personal grounds alone—about the harm he might do if his energies were not harnessed to a task. So he dangled the Washington Embassy; and, himself about to visit President Roosevelt, suggested that Beaverbrook should accompany him. Beaverbrook declined the invitation.

On 17 June, on a day when the full extent of the defeat in Libya was becoming apparent, when the fearsome spectre of a retreat to the Nile arose, Beaverbrook spoke to the 1922 Committee—the Conservative Party caucus. He was warmly received. Members told him that they had not wished him to leave the Government, that he was the only man as dynamic as Churchill. He could not but be pleased by such praise from a quarter which, in the past, had looked on him with so much suspicion. On the morning of this meeting, A. J. Cummings had remarked in the *News Chronicle* that the rumour that Beaverbrook would rejoin the War Cabinet grew, causing fear in political circles who disliked "the second coming of this flaming meteor. Now all is well. The comet has passed on." That day, Churchill left by air for Washington. Before going he wrote to the King: "In the case of my death on this journey I . . . advise that you should entrust the formation of a new Government to Mr. Anthony Eden."[4]

Thus one political problem was settled, as far as it lay within the power of a single individual to settle it.

# CHAPTER XII

# *"The monstrous iteration
of events"*

*The Middle East is a crossroads where everything
passes—religions, armies, empires, trade routes—but
nothing changes.*
—Charles de Gaulle

*There will be no retreat. The fate of Prussia is at stake.*
—Helmut von Moltke at Königgrätz, 1866

SUDDENLY, ON 21 JUNE, the brooding political crisis in
Britain became acute. The fortress of Tobruk, as *The
Times* was calling it the day before, fell to a German attack
which lasted twenty-four hours. Its garrison of 30,000
were made prisoners. Delighted by the victory, Hitler
called off the preparations for the final assault on Malta.
Raeder's "Great Plan" could, he thought, succeed with-
out the capture of the island. On 1 July, he persuaded
Mussolini to send troops reserved for Malta to the
Egyptian battle-front. On that same day, as it chanced,
a debate of crucial importance opened in the British
Parliament. On 25 June a motion had been placed on the
order paper of the House of Commons in the name of Sir
John Wardlaw-Milne, a greatly respected Conservative
M.P. It called for a vote of censure on the Government.
Discontent with Churchill's conduct of the war, long
gathering, had at last come to a head.

In the grand perspective of the war, the fall of Tobruk was not a military disaster of the first order. But the fact is—and it is easily explained—that the news of the surrender was the bitterest day in the whole war for millions of people in Britain. Why? Why did that pleasant June day (as it was in London) seem to have so little warmth in its sunshine? Why were the gardens, in that wonderful summer for roses, so little able to console their owners? Because Tobruk had, during 1941, defied every attempt by the enemy to take it during an isolation which lasted for 230 days. And now it had fallen in a matter of hours. What was the explanation?

Did it mean that the enemy's margin of superiority in the quality and numbers of weapons had widened? Did it mean that the morale of the Eighth Army was not as high as once it had been? During those hours of gloom and anger when the tidings from Tobruk struck Britain, it was impossible to be sure what was the truth.

Five months earlier, the Commander-in-Chief in the Middle East had decided that never again must Tobruk be held as an isolated fortress. In consequence its defences had been neglected. Its minefields were breached. The anti-tank ditch was, in part, filled with sand. Its artillery control system was dismantled. Tobruk was no longer a fortress.

The intentions of the British command, after the decisive defeat of the Eighth Army at "Knightsbridge", had therefore been to give up Tobruk as part of the general withdrawal to Egypt. The Prime Minister signalled, "Presume there is no question in any case of giving up Tobruk", but Auchinleck, with whom the decision rested, had decided that on no account must the Eighth Army or any part of it be invested in the town. He summoned reinforcements from Syria to the western frontier of Egypt so that the Eighth Army should be free to continue the battle as a mobile "field army" with Tobruk as the secure flank.

However, in the turmoil of the swiftly moving battle, Rommel was in a position to isolate Tobruk before Auchinleck in Cairo could realize what was happening and order an immediate and complete evacuation of the town. In any case, the conduct of the retreat should have been in the hands of the commander in the field. But at this moment a twofold misunderstanding seems to have existed. General Ritchie, Commander of the Eighth Army, thought that the Commander-in-Chief in Cairo was ordering him to hold Rommel west of Tobruk—by this time an impossible task. And Churchill was applauding by cable a supposed decision that Ritchie "would leave as many troops in Tobruk as are necessary to hold the place for certain".

As Churchill must have known of the January decision not to attempt to hold Tobruk permanently, his reiterated insistence that it should be held may be explained either because he feared the effect on the nation's sensitive morale of a failure to defend it, or because, in moments of disappointment, he showed distrust of a supposed lack of fighting spirit in his commanders. Himself an enthusiast for all the complexities of modern warfare, he was nevertheless apt to see a battle in the simple, old categories of so many "rifles", "sabres", etc. Besides, Churchill was, after all, not simply a strategist; he was the supreme leader of a nation at war. Over the spirit of his followers he must anxiously and assiduously watch. "Lions led by donkeys?" The British armies in the Second World War were rather lions led by a lion. What was lacking was, perhaps, a touch of the serpent.

And so the indefensible was defended and the hardest blow of all the war fell on the British people—and on its leader. Churchill heard the news in circumstances that made it all the harder to bear. He and Sir Alan Brooke, Chief of the Imperial General Staff, were standing beside

President Roosevelt's desk in the White House when General Marshall entered with a pink piece of paper. It bore the crushing news.

The Prime Minister could not doubt that his political fortune was now in the balance as it had not been at any time since 1916. He had no need to read the *New York Herald Tribune,* whose London correspondent reported next day "every London newspaper plans to use the word 'disaster' ". That night he telephoned to Eden in London reporting that the New York newspapers were full of the impending fall of the Government. Eden had heard nothing of it: much grief, he reported, "but nothing has happened to shake us". It seemed, at the time, an optimistic view.


On that day, a few hours earlier, there had been an impressive demonstration in Birmingham. Over the Town Hall floated the Red Flag with the hammer and sickle. Ten thousand workers and Home Guards marched in procession with music and banners; as they passed the platform from which speeches were to be delivered, many of them gave the clenched-fist salute of the Communists.

In the end 30,000 people filled the square in front of the municipal buildings. It was the eve of the first anniversary of Hitler's attack on Russia and the rally was intended to testify to Britain's solidarity with her ally. Mr. William Barkley, of the *Daily Express,* was standing among the reporters when news reached him that Tobruk had fallen. Barkley had come to Birmingham because the chief speaker was the proprietor of his newspaper.

At the moment when Lord Beaverbrook was mounting the rostrum where the Union Jack and the Red Flag were sewn together, Barkley whispered to him the news that had arrived. Whether Beaverbrook was already aware of it or not he could not judge, although Barkley thought that for a second a glazed look came into the older man's eyes. A few minutes later, Beaverbrook was addressing the crowd in his urgent, dramatic style.

They were, he told them, "the warriors of the old world". They had been promised a Second Front; now the need was for urgency. "You will drive German industry elsewhere by bombing. But you have no right to believe that the bomber will bring the war to an end. Back to the British Army! The time has come to give out all we have got!" The meeting ended with the Internationale sung fervently by thousands who would not know about the disaster in Libya until a few minutes after midnight.

There it was next morning, on the first pages of the newspapers. The writer of the leading article in *The Times* shook his head in dismay: "incontestably a disaster".

In Washington, Churchill would imagine the headlines, the storm-signals in the House of Commons, "anxious for a statement", the perturbation of the public. "Not since the fall of Singapore," said the London Letter of the *Manchester Guardian*, "has there been so much expression of public feeling. The difference in that feeling is now anger and irritation rather than dismay and depression." The anger lost none of its sharpness through the coincidence that the fall of Tobruk was announced in newspapers which recalled that exactly a year had passed since Hitler opened his attack on Russia.

Would the Government fall, however? That was the question that most nearly affected Churchill, 3,000 miles away in Washington, lapped in sympathy and good comradeship in the White House and dependent for his impressions on telegrams and telephones, those profoundly unsatisfying oracles in moments of crisis. The omens were doubtful.

On the one hand the widespread annoyance over

Britain's military misfortunes was reflected in a fresh outbreak of criticism. Men looked with a harder eye and
spoke with a tarter tongue about their rulers. There was,
however, no discernible alternative to the Government.
"True, there is a considerable section of the Tory Party
that intensely dislikes Mr. Churchill. But as patriots, they
are not in the least likely to vote him out if it involves any
risk to the country."[1]


"Vote him out?" It seemed that this was precisely what
the House of Commons was invited to do. There it was,
printed in the Parliamentary papers: over the names of Sir
John Wardlaw-Milne, Admiral of the Fleet Sir Roger
Keyes, and Mr. Hore-Belisha, former Secretary of State
for War: "That the House, while paying tribute to the
heroism and endurance of the Armed Forces of the
Crown in circumstances of extreme difficulty, has no confidence in the central direction of the war." The House of
Commons was being invited to declare Churchill's Government—and above all Churchill himself—incompetent.

American observers reported the Parliamentary drama.
That the atmosphere of the House was more electric than
at any time since the fall of France[2] was the verdict of the
*New York Herald Tribune's* correspondent, who did not,
however, predict a Parliamentary disaster for Churchill.

The *New York Times* correspondent, Raymond Daniell,
thought (24 June) that Wardlaw-Milne's frontal attack
was premature, and that Attlee had taken a quick political
advantage of this unwary opponent. Churchill's more
responsible critics wished him to stop doubling the roles
of Prime Minister and chief strategist. But it was doubtful
if, even now, he could change his ways. And was it desirable? Those who were inside the strategy-making machine
were convinced that a major war must be controlled by a

Prime Minister, closely geared to the Chiefs of Staff, as Churchill was.

It seemed, however, that the fall of Tobruk had provided air with which a host of dissatisfactions could fill their lungs. In the fourth year of the war Britain's armament still lagged behind the enemy's in quality and design. Why? If imperial resources were inadequate to hold Singapore, it was assumed that one reason was that guns and tanks of the latest pattern were being poured into Egypt. What became of this assumption now?

At this time, Beaverbrook saw his old enemy Ernest Bevin and began a discussion about the nature of the Government that would succeed Churchill's were the Prime Minister to fall. According to Bevin, on whose reported recollections of the interview this account depends, Beaverbrook thought that Churchill's Government was in danger. Thereafter—but what may have been in Beaverbrook's mind does not clearly emerge. Bevin would not allow him to go on. He told Churchill what had happened. And Churchill did not believe him.[3]

Bevin was incapable of inventing this incident, although quite capable of misinterpreting it. He had, too, a strong desire to make sure that Beaverbrook was not brought back into the Government. Churchill *was* in acute political danger. In such circumstances Beaverbrook, whose mind had a strong melodramatic cast, would be liable to swing in judgment from sunshine to shadow. And, being the restless, resourceful man he was, he might well want to look at all the possibilities of the situation. If Churchill fell, who would follow him? Ernie? John? Anthony? He would wish to know what was going on in the minds of other men. This was completely in the character of Beaverbrook the politician or of Beaverbrook the journalist. As Herbert Morrison said shrewdly of him, "Max, you are a very simple-minded Machiavelli."

Be that as it may, Bevin went away convinced that Beaverbrook had sought to draw him into an intrigue against Churchill. He shared his conviction with his associates. But had Beaverbrook really been guilty of anything that could be called disloyalty? Events, more persuasive than opinion, supplied the answer in a few days.

Five days after the fall of Tobruk, an important by-election occurred in the Maldon division of Essex. The seat was a piece of Tory Party property and its possession would not have been disputed under the usual conditions of party truce. Sir Evelyn Ruggles-Brise, whose death caused the vacancy, had held it in the last general election with a majority of 7,800. However, neither the time nor the circumstances were usual. Towards the end of May, the *Evening Standard* had informed its readers that Mr. Thomas Driberg, who edited the William Hickey diary in the *Daily Express*, had accepted an invitation to stand as an independent candidate.

Mr. Driberg was an unusually gifted man of thirty-seven, with versatile qualifications; a scholar as well as a journalist, a lucid and accomplished speaker. He lived in the constituency, and, as an Anglican, served as a church-warden in the village church of Bradwell-juxta-Mare. Campaigning as "a candid friend for Churchill" and "the local man with the national reputation", he could be expected to make a dual impact.

He had already, in the William Hickey diary, written derisively about those who sought to discourage independent candidates in war-time on the ground, for example, that, "since electoral registers were incomplete, democracy could not utter a true opinion in any constituency". "A breathtaking remark from a supporter of the party machine," said Hickey-Driberg, "and a dangerous one, since the Government also has won quite a number of by-elections."

Writing to the electors from his home at Bradwell-juxta-Mare, Driberg now made an adroit defence of the role of independent Members of Parliament in war-time. "It is worth noting," he said, "that the Second Front campaign now triumphantly endorsed . . . began in independent . . . quarters, not in official Government parties and organs. I stand as an independent candidate. . . . Sometimes I may be ranged with such Conservative critics of the Government at Sir John Wardlaw-Milne, or such Labour representatives as Mr. Shinwell."

Driberg was casting his electoral net widely. He was, in hard political fact, a left-wing socialist intellectual who, in his election address, gave general assent to a programme including "transfer to common ownership of services, industries and companies in which managerial inefficiency or the profit motive is harming the war effort". He was, however, far too astute a propagandist to lay stress exclusively on a single note of appeal, or to neglect the heaven-sent political advantage of the disaster in the Western Desert. One of his leaflets, headed "Tragedy at Tobruk", opened: "Something has gone wrong in Libya again . . . Something is wrong indeed, *near the top*."

He promised the electors to expose racketeers who make high profits "while our boys die in Libya" and "to keep always in close touch with you".

He was cheered on his way by a message from George Bernard Shaw, who insisted that the party truce did not mean "a corrupt bargain between the two parties to vote just as they did last time. It means dropping the party lines and voting for the ablest candidate. It not only means that independent candidates are quite in order, but that the official party candidates are entirely out of order."

The Maldon division of Essex contains four towns and

about fifty villages, which the candidates covered in their loudspeaker cars in brilliant sunny weather. Driberg's campaign gained from the shrewd advice and vitalizing enthusiasm of Sir Richard Acland, whose recipe for success was "nine days of preparation and five days of electioneering". He also enjoyed the support of a local clergyman, the Rev. K. J. M. Boggis, who was sub-Dean of Bocking and Secretary of the Braintree Labour Party. Mr. Boggis defied the disapproval of Labour headquarters to join in the fight; so did a local Communist.

As the campaign went on excitement mounted, and when Driberg arrived at ten o'clock for the open-air eve-of-the-poll meeting in Braintree, he found a crowd of six or seven thousand. The atmosphere was electric.

The end of what the Prime Minister called "an unnecessary and meaningless contest" was spectacular. Driberg won Maldon by 6,000, an apparent turnover of 13,000 votes. It was an extraordinary achievement, indicating a high degree of emotion and political instability in the country.

His majority, thought *The Times*, had certainly been swollen by the recent disasters or, as the *Manchester Guardian* put it, "the sudden national anger at the [Tobruk] defeat had the opportunity in Maldon as nowhere else of relieving itself". It spoke of Driberg as the member for Mersa Matruh (a place which had been prominent in the North African fighting).

It was the fourth—and heaviest—electoral defeat for the Government since March, and, with a critical debate in the House of Commons at hand, not a cheerful omen for Churchill, then approaching the Clyde in the co-pilot's seat of a flying boat.

"This seemed to me to be a bad time"—but after brooding for a little over the news in his train going south the Prime Minister fell asleep. "What a blessing is the gift of sleep! The War Cabinet were on the platform to greet me."[4] In fact, the reception he received at Euston was more than chilly. As A. J. Cummings had predicted a few days earlier: "This time Mr. Churchill will come back from the United States to a nation angered as well as disturbed."[5]

On his introduction to the House of Commons, Mr. Driberg was sponsored by two independent members, Mr. Vernon Bartlett and Sir Richard Acland. The new M.P. had arrived just in time to cast his vote in a momentous division.

On 1 July, on the morning of the censure debate, *The Times* focussed the controversy on a single question: "How a great and inventive industrial country nearing the end of a third year of war has failed to supply its army with weapons superior to those employed by the enemy." But this was to over-simplify the matter, as the newspaper's letter column showed. For more was at issue than questions of supply. There was strategy—and the strategists. There was the overall supervision of the war—and the machinery for controlling it. "The vast majority of M.P.s oppose him (Churchill) as Minister of Defence". wrote Sir John Marriott. "Let him test the opinion of Parliament."

The reading of the British intelligentsia had been sombre that weekend as the reviews distributed warning and blame. Whitehall was at fault: so was Cairo. Armour and fire-power alike were inadequate, mourned the editorial writer in the *New Statesman* under the grim heading "Inquest on Disaster". And what was the use of boasting of America's vast production when we were simply repeating ill-designed types by mass production? The writer went on to draw a chilling picture of a possible—and near —future in which the German strategists, exploiting their command of the Mediterranean and their short sea communications, might be content to hold the Russians "while they fling a good part of their storm-troops at objectives which range from Batum to Suez and the Middle Eastern oilfields". His conclusion was that, while the desert generals might have failed us, "the suspicion of obstinacy and incompetence goes higher".[6]

*The Spectator* laid its emphasis on a reported failure in generalship and gave warning that "any attempt at excuse or exoneration would have disastrous effects on the Government politically".

An officer, whose letter was quoted in *The Economist*, lent his support to their opinion. "Tobruk," he said, "has done more to undermine confidence in the Army command than all the *Daily Mirror* could possibly say." Seeking to explain why Tobruk was so much graver a blow politically than it was in the military sense, *The Economist* said: "It is the monstrous iteration of events like these that eats into confidence."

The dismal ironies of vast production and second-rate quality in "the ring of steel" round Germany of which Harry Hopkins had been speaking in New York at the very moment Tobruk was falling—these were glanced at. But this was above all a crisis of leadership with an acuteness all its own, and "Mr. Churchill is still the only possible leader; and a Parliament which sought to bring him down might well bring down Parliament itself". Here, bluntly uncovered, was the explosive core of the crisis. One hand at least would not have flinched from detonating the charge. In *Tribune*, Aneurin Bevan wrote, "It is time to cut down the tree [Churchill] and let in the light".

But was it time? Or was *The Economist* right in pointing to Churchill as the only possible leader, whose destruction could not be attempted by Parliament without endangering the whole Parliamentary fabric? "Indispensable." The adjective can quickly acquire a bitter flavour.

Sir Osbert Sitwell wrote greatly to the point[7] the day before Tobruk fell: "When the public begins to say of a leader, 'But who could possibly replace him?' it means that the possibility is occupying the public mind and that change is coming."

What was in the public mind, "naturally perplexed and rightly angry",[8] as well it might be in the last days of June, on the grave issue of the national leadership? On this question there is objective evidence which, while it may be regarded with some caution, cannot be ignored.

At regular intervals throughout the war, the popular support for the Prime Minister and his Government was measured by the Gallup Poll. A "representative cross-section" of the public was asked

(1) Do you approve or disapprove of Mr. Churchill as Prime Minister?

(2) Are you satisfied or dissatisfied with the Government's conduct of the war?

When the results of these enquiries are displayed as a graph, two facts are immediately visible: Churchill's prestige with the people was at all times superior to that of his Government. The margin in his favour varied from time to time. But the variation was on the whole due to the greater sharpness of the rise and fall in the favour enjoyed by the Government, as compared with the steadier esteem in which the Prime Minister was held.

This latter is shown by an almost horizontal line, moving across the paper within the limits of a narrow belt, gently undulating between ninety-two and eighty per cent of the recorded opinions. Only once did approval fall below the eighty mark. That was in the poll which reflected public feeling just after the fall of Tobruk. Broadly speaking, throughout 1941 and 1942 Churchill was twice as popular as his Government.

When disaster struck, public displeasure was, it seems,

vented on the administration more severely than on its
leader. Thus, in May 1942, before Tobruk, over sixty per
cent approved of ministers' conduct of the war; but two
months later, after Tobruk, approval was given by only
forty per cent. Over the same period, the fall in public
approval of Churchill was only half as heavy.

It may seem illogical of the people to blame a Government for strategic disasters more heavily than the man
who insisted on—who gloried in—his monopoly of
strategy. But logic is one thing; wisdom is another.

The people must have known that for military errors
Churchill, more than any other man, was responsible.
After all, they knew that he was Minister of Defence. But
they realized instinctively that, as Leon Trotsky told the
military delegates at the 11th Congress of the Bolshevik
Party, "War is no science; it is a savage and bloody art".[9]
They were looking for a captain whom they could trust
to stay with them in the fight until the clock struck twelve,
and five minutes later. Heart, fibre, pride, passion—these
and not strategical insight were the tests which led them
to Churchill (who had other gifts as well).

It was, in a peculiar sense, *his* war, *his* mission, and he
would give himself completely to it. Blunders? If they
existed they had illustrious precedent and excuse. "I have
so often in my life been mistaken that I no longer blush
for it."[10] If they had ever heard this remark of Napoleon,
the British would have acknowledged it grimly as belonging inevitably to the muddled business of war. They would
cling to Churchill until irretrievable disaster befell or until
a leader of greater stature appeared.

The Prime Minister knew that he had the loyalty of the
people. Parliament knew it. And the Ministers knew that
on them would fall, unjustly as it might be, the knout of
popular annoyance.

This did not mean, however, that Churchill approached

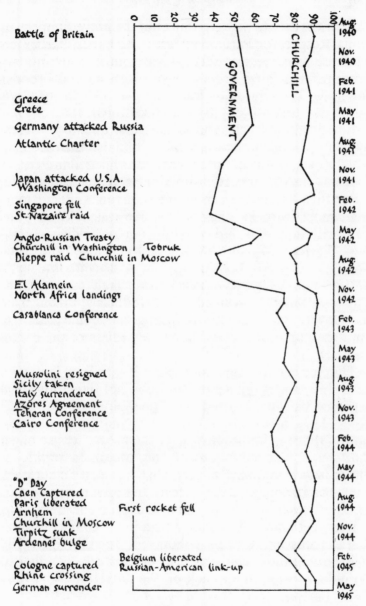

Battle of Britain

Greece
Crete
Germany attacked Russia

Atlantic Charter

Japan attacked U.S.A.
Washington Conference

Singapore fell
St. Nazaire raid

Anglo-Russian Treaty
Churchill in Washington | Tobruk
Dieppe raid  Churchill in Moscow

El Alamein
North Africa landings

Casablanca Conference

Mussolini resigned
Sicily taken
Italy surrendered
Azores Agreement
Teheran Conference
Cairo Conference

"D" Day
Caen Captured
Paris liberated
Arnhem                    First rocket fell
Churchill in Moscow
Tirpitz sunk
Ardennes bulge

                          Belgium liberated
Cologne captured          Russian-American link-up
Rhine crossing
German surrender

GOVERNMENT

CHURCHILL

Aug. 1940
Nov. 1940
Feb. 1941
May 1941
Aug. 1941
Nov. 1941
Feb. 1942
May 1942
Aug. 1942
Nov. 1942
Feb. 1943
May 1943
Aug. 1943
Nov. 1943
Feb. 1944
May 1944
Aug. 1944
Nov. 1944
Feb. 1945
May 1945

*by kind permission of the National Opinion Poll*

the critical debate with anything but the gravest apprehensions. Respect for Parliament was in his bones. Parliament was the tawdry, imperfect—but somehow glorious—flower of a historic process over which he had brooded for long. The schoolboy humour of the House of Commons, its lack of dignity, its occasional rancour and irresponsibility, its clumsiness as an instrument of government—none of these things could diminish the deference he felt for it, or the infinite precautions he used towards it.

It was the ultimate repository of power in the land. He knew this, better than most men, having suffered more than most from its disapproval. He was told on good authority that he would certainly win in the division lobbies. Sir John Wardlaw-Milne had misjudged the situation, had, perhaps, been trapped by Attlee into issuing an untimely challenge on which he was likely to be beaten. The newspapers, it seemed, withheld their approval from the Government but shrank from giving countenance to an attack upon it pressed home regardless of the consequences.

The Tory centre, heirs of the old Bonar Law feud with Churchill, might rejoice in the lobbies of the House. But how many of them would translate their glee into hostile votes? How many would risk destroying the administration of the man whose hold over the people was stronger than theirs? The main body of Tory Members would—as the *Manchester Guardian* predicted—give stolid support, while the Labour Party, whatever the private views of its members, would be loyal to the Government.

Emanuel Shinwell remained firm in his conviction that the war was being badly conducted, but that Churchill was, among those available, the best man to conduct it. Would he join in the attack on the Government? Churchill's Parliamentary Private Secretary, Brigadier George Harvie-Watt, spoke to him in the Lobby of the House

"The Chief has a lot of worry just now. He doesn't deserve to be annoyed by attacks in the House. You mustn't forget that the Prime Minister has great military gifts. His ancestor was the Duke of Marlborough."

"If military genius can be handed down like that," Shinwell retorted, "then I should be a good critic. My ancestor was Moses."

On the whole, it seemed that the descendant of Moses would not smash the tables of the law in wrath when he came down from Mount Sinai.

All this was comforting enough to the man who had flown back over the Atlantic to face prosecution in the court which, above all others, he feared. But, as he knew very well, it was not enough to score a substantial victory when heads were counted in the division lobbies. The whips, of course, would furnish him with a majority. That was their job. But Chamberlain had been overthrown while he still had a majority of eighty in the House. It was necessary for the Government to win the argument as well as the votes, to demonstrate that they had a better case than their critics; that he, Churchill, was at the head of a group of men superior in vision and energy to any alternative.

Anxious in spirit over a political danger, as he was not before or afterwards during the whole course of the war, Churchill made ready his defences against the assault. He could not be faulted for lack of alacrity or thoroughness: he would fight. He would not yield an inch. He would give no quarter.

Meanwhile the British Army in Africa was bundling in the direction of the Nile delta with Rommel hard on its heels. Secret papers were burning in embassy gardens in Cairo. The rich were fleeing. Railway station platforms were thronged. On 1 July, while the orators in London were brushing up their speeches for the debate in the

House next day, the Afrika Korps radio warned the ladies of Alexandria: "Make ready to receive us!" Rommel knew that the picture was not quite so bright as that message suggested. He had only twenty-six tanks that could move. And his Italian troops were tired. Moreover, the British had fallen back to an admirable position to make a stand, at El Alamein, with the sea to the north and the cliffs of the Qattâra Depression to the south.

Thirteen hundred miles away, in another continent, the long-awaited main German offensive had burst on the Russian front at Kursk on 21 June. Eleven Panzer divisions moved eastwards over the steppes. On 30 June, the attack widened towards the south below Kharkov. The First Panzer Army crossed the Donetz. Dust raised by the tanks, smoke from the blazing villages—a vast curtain of man-made fog marked the victorious, irresistible flood of the Germans sweeping eastwards towards the Volga and soon to reach southwards towards the Caspian. "We shall soon see each other," wrote one German soldier to his wife. "All of us feel that the end, Victory, is near."

In his operations-room behind the Ruweisat Ridge, Auchinleck, Commander-in-Chief Middle East, sensitive to every move of Rommel's, could not ignore the enormous convulsion to the north, the splintering of the Russian front. The *Wehrmacht* was moving on his rear, on the oil of Iraq and Persia—safeguarded by British armies, which existed mainly on paper. His anxieties were enormous. He dealt coolly with the one that was nearest.

In the first breathless week of July 1942, Hitler's war had arrived at its climax. Sir John Wardlaw-Milne offered to postpone the debate in the House. Churchill refused.

# CHAPTER XIII

# *The thirteenth stroke of a crazy clock*

*He spoke as a man should speak, because he felt as a man should feel in such circumstances.*
— Hazlitt on Chatham

SUMMONING HIS LEGIONS to the defence of the citadel, Churchill turned to Lord Beaverbrook.

The Canadian, after being for some time a restless force in the Government, had elbowed his way out of it. Since then, he had teased and mystified the public in Britain and America about his intentions. He was known to hold independent opinions on strategy and to have conducted a running, unequal fight with Ernest Bevin. His Second Front agitation, borrowed from the Communists, at once urged the Government forward and jostled it on the way. He was suspected by some of intriguing against Churchill and of coveting the highest post in the land. It could, more accurately, be said that he allowed others to spread rumours about him which would at least remind the Cabinet of his existence.

He was idle; busy with trifles; dissatisfied; the owner of great power which in the circumstances of war he could not fully wield. Churchill looked on him with comprehension and, sometimes, with alarm. However, it is unlikely that Churchill had the slightest doubt what Beaverbrook's answer would be to an appeal for help in a dire emergency.

After thirty years of stormy friendship, sometimes frayed but never broken, the two men knew one another.

When Churchill's call for help came on the Sunday of the Prime Minister's return from the United States, it swept away for Beaverbrook a whole swarm of smaller promptings. Here was an issue of the simple, rough-hewn sort he liked, a call to battle rousing his spirit, an appeal for help pleasing to his vanity, a summons to loyalty, his favourite among the virtues, a rescue from boredom.

He instantly put out of his mind any ambitions, pre-occupations or interests that may have been there. He asked the Prime Minister if he could have access to any secret information he might need. This being granted, he went to work with his usual enthusiasm. Emissaries, with his delegated power of enquiry, moved into various Government offices, where they and their enquiries were received with some lack of eagerness. However, they obtained the information they wanted.

Beaverbrook was not the only old companion-in-arms to whom Churchill turned in the crisis. There was also Mr. Robert Boothby, M.P., to whom he had not addressed a word since 1941, when Boothby had resigned his post as Parliamentary Secretary to the Ministry of Food. Boothby had been one of Churchill's closest political associates, Churchill's Parliamentary Private Secretary when he was Chancellor of the Exchequer, and one of the thirty-three Conservative Members of Parliament who had voted against Chamberlain. But in June 1940 the two men quarrelled.

Later a Select Committee decided that Boothby had acted in a way inconsistent with Parliamentary standards in his pre-war advocacy of bringing pressure on Germany to release the assets of Czech refugees because he did not disclose that he had a personal financial interest in this cause. The "interest" consisted of a loan from a Czech refugee, repaid in full. Convinced that he had acted with complete propriety, Boothby particularly resented the fact that Churchill never gave him the opportunity for a full, private explanation of his conduct before sending him out into the political wilderness.

On the day of the censure debate on the fall of Tobruk, Boothby was in the dining-room of the House of Commons when the Prime Minister waved to him to come over. Churchill asked: "Are you in favour of the Government?"

"Of course," said Boothby. "There is no alternative."

Churchill then put another question: "Are you in favour of me?"

"Yes," replied Boothby, "although you have done me great harm."

"Will you speak for us this afternoon?"

And Boothby said: "Yes."

Without any more ado, Churchill led Boothby to the Speaker, Captain FitzRoy, and said: "Mr. Boothby will speak this afternoon." Afterwards, in the smoking-room, he drank a toast "to the Pegasus wings of Bob's oratory". But he did not talk to Boothby again until the war was over. Later, Boothby looked back on the incident with understanding and without bitterness. In a crisis which was both Parliamentary and national, he had been mobilized to play his part; it was not a time for indulging in sentiment.[1] "L'ingratitude est la preuve de l'homme de caractère."[2]

Meanwhile the whips were whittling assiduously at the tree of insurrection and Sir John Wardlaw-Milne was soon to pay a sardonic tribute to their success. Some of the most pertinacious gadflies of the Ministers—men like Shinwell—would not take part in this debate. They would, at most, abstain from voting. And the 1922 Committee, the Tory Parliamentary caucus, gave warning to Sir John that it strongly disapproved of the whole enterprise of a censure motion. Sir John, although Chairman of the Foreign Affairs Committee and the National Expenditure Committee, was very much a lone wolf in the strongly critical line he took on the conduct of the war.

Outside, it was a summer afternoon of sunshine and cloud; the weather was not so warm as it had been. Inside the Chamber, the benches and galleries were more crowded than they had been on any afternoon since the Norway debate which brought Neville Chamberlain down. The atmosphere was electric. Sir John Wardlaw-Milne, tall, dignified, wearing a light-grey summer suit, rose in his place. Born in Elgin and brought up in Helensburgh, he had retained, after years in the East as a "box wallah", an agreeable West of Scotland intonation.

The aim of Sir John and his supporters that afternoon was, not to unseat the Prime Minister, but to reduce his authority by ensuring that he shared the direction of the war with a War Cabinet under whom a "supreme commander" would co-ordinate the work and requirements of the three services. He thought, then and later, that it would be better if Churchill, the nation's saviour, ceased to be Minister of Defence.

It was as certain as could be that Churchill would reject any diminution of his powers, but, as an outcome of the debate, Sir John might achieve an underlying purpose close to his heart: to bring home to the House that the Army was neglected and the supply of munitions uncoordinated. A sense that injustice was being done to the Army gave impetus to his Parliamentary action and led him into an early, and almost fatal, blunder.

Sir John's speech that day has usually been regarded as a disaster which stifled the debate at birth. The reason was this. After speaking impressively for a quarter of an hour or so, he was inspired to interject that it might be a good idea to appoint the Duke of Gloucester Commander-in-Chief of the British Army—"without, of course, administrative duties". The House of Commons greeted the proposal with unconcealed delight. Churchill threw his hands up in the air in triumph. As one Member thought, it was as if he had just heard that Rommel had been captured in the desert. And tradition says that the debate, shaken at the moment by an earthquake of derision, did not fully recover its gravity.

A. P. Herbert, who sat in the House as Petty Officer Herbert, was reminded of a remark of his father's: "Sir, your last observation was like the thirteenth stroke of a crazy clock which not only is itself discredited but casts a shade of doubt over all previous assertions."

It seemed likely that some of those who listened to Sir John did not hear him to the end of the sentence and that others, who did, seized on a heavent-sent opportunity to wreck the speech. In any event, the attack on the central conduct of the war suffered. From Sir John's point of view, his ill-advised interpolation of a frivolous matter was a great misfortune. He had some things to say that deserved the attention of the House.

The cause of Britain's military failures, he argued, lay not in Libya but in London, not with the generals in the field but with the initial, vital mistake of combining the offices of Prime Minister and Minister of Defence. He asked the House to consider what a Prime Minister had to do in wartime, the demands made on him by the changes which the war was bringing about in the nation's life, the proliferation of new ministries, the conscription to work of young and old, production problems, the need for close relations with Dominions, Colonies and allies.

The task of the Minister of Defence was different, involving close and constant supervision of the strategic plans for which he had obtained the sanction of the War

Cabinet. This called for a strong man—Sir John repeated the adjective four times in one minute—strong enough to see that his generals, admirals and air-marshals were not interfered with unduly from above. Other nations had found one man to control their armed forces. The Japanese had found an admiral, the Germans a general. "There seems no reason why we should not do so also."

By combining the two sets of duties of which he had spoken, Britain had suffered in both fields. "We have suffered from the want of the closest examination by the Prime Minister of what is going on here at home and also by the want of that direction which we should get from the Minister of Defence."

Complaining of the lack of information about the disasters in Singapore and Burma, Sir John said that he had no doubt why the former was lost: Britain had depended on American sea-power to defend her positions in the Far East. Why, he asked, were more Indian troops not sent to the Far East? Why could we not have sent the five hundred planes to Malaya which would have made all the difference?

He passed on to Libya: "What is wrong with our plans, our strategy or our production which puts us into this inferior position?" Britain was turning out quantities of munitions, aeroplanes, guns. Why were they not in the right place at the right time?

The Prime Minister had excused Singapore by saying that priority had been given to the Nile valley. It was untrue, inaccurate, the Prime Minister had been completely misled. "We have almost got to the stage when if my right honourable friend comes down to the House to tell us we are going to win, one becomes almost afraid of what we shall hear next."

Turning to the question of guns and tanks, he denounced their inadequacy in numbers and quality: what

excuse had the Government for urging the public to produce weapons that were out of date? One Chairman had
succeeded another on the Tank Board, meeting once a
month for two hours and departing, rewarded with
knighthoods.

Lord Beaverbrook had said in February that we had a
good supply of six-pounder guns, capable of penetrating
the armour of any tank ever built and now in excellent
production. After the recent Libyan campaign, would
anyone confirm that now? The gun was known before the
war, but only came into production in spate in January
1942. Our tanks were destroyed in Libya by a "surprise
weapon", the German 88-mm. gun—first used in Spain in
January 1937!

After weapons came operations. Who gave the decision
for the capitulation of Tobruk and who previously attempted to hold it? Was the decision made upon the
battlefield, in Cairo, in London or in Washington? This
was indeed a grave charge. Nobody could doubt at whom
it was aimed. Churchill had been in Washington when
Tobruk fell.

Sir John returned to his main theme, the need for one
man, giving his whole time to winning the war and in
complete charge of all the armed forces. Such a man
should not be the Prime Minister and should probably—
unless Sir John had failed to convey his meaning clearly
—be a soldier or a sailor. The heroic leader of the nation
was pouring out his spirit in matters for which he had no
particular talent.

Within a few minutes of Sir John resuming his seat at
the end of a speech which had barely survived total disaster, his unyielding argument was completely neutralized
by the man who seconded his motion. Admiral of the
Fleet Sir Roger Keyes, v.c., who, in the uniform of an
Admiral of the Fleet, had made an impressive—perhaps

decisive—intervention in the Norway debate two years earlier.

Whether proposer and seconder had consulted one another about the drastic changes of policy they meant to urge may be doubted. It seems likely that the two main advocates of more closely organized conduct of the war were themselves guilty of an elementary failure in staff-work.

Speaking with all the lustre of his heroism at Zeebrugge a quarter of a century earlier, all the authority of his rank and experience, and all the bitterness of a man who, in his indomitable old age, had been driven from his post at the head of the Commandos, Keyes dismissed as false the idea that the Prime Minister rode rough-shod over his service advisers and took the whole direction of the war into his own hands. Masterful he was, impatient of criticism, with a preference for men who agreed with his judgment, but he would never undertake any enterprise for which his Chiefs of Staff were not prepared to accept responsibility.

It was the Chiefs of Staff, it seemed, and not the Prime Minister, who had failed to bundle the Italians out of North Africa in 1941 when this could have been done; they rather than Churchill who had been "blind to the immediate and immense advantages of shortening the route to the Middle East"; they who had failed to insist that the air defences of Crete should be developed when that island had been providentially presented to us by Italy's attack on Greece; they who had neglected the golden chance of capturing Trondheim, of building up commando forces in the Mediterranean. Now they had sent the *Repulse* and the *Prince of Wales* uselessly, foolishly, to inevitable destruction in the Far East. It was a record for which the Navy would never forgive the Admiralty. For certainly the Prime Minister would not have sent the ships there on his own authority against naval advice.

"It is hard," cried the gallant old sailor, "that three times in the Prime Minister's career he should have been thwarted—in Gallipoli, in Norway and in the Mediterranean—in carrying out strategical strokes which might have altered the whole course of the war, each time because his constitutional naval advisers declined to share the responsibility with him if it entailed risk."

Having roamed too widely, having—like an amateur general—allowed personal feelings to influence him too much, having dispersed his attack and weakened his impact, Keyes sought in the closing minutes of his speech to marshal his forces for a final effort.

He had been told that the motion was bad political tactics. He was not concerned with political tactics, but it was intolerable to watch the war machine lumbering from one disaster to another through failure of nerve at the Admiralty and an obsession, hag-riding the Air Ministry, that they could win the war by bombing alone.

The Prime Minister was his friend, his political godfather, who had persuaded him to come into the House eight years before on a simple programme: to restore Britain's sea-power and her naval aviation. Now he saw him surrounded by Ministers without courage or ability, a Home Secretary who set strikers free, a Minister of Labour who once led strikes and now could not stop them, a First Lord who was responsible for naval disarmament. In singling out these three for special condemnation, Keyes was guilty of extraordinary political ineptitude. For each of the three was a Labour Minister.

In conclusion, he said that he wanted to see the Prime Minister putting his house in order and, at the head of a real national Government, rallying the country once again!

Sir John Wardlaw-Milne had made a damaging tactical error; now Sir Roger Keyes was guilty of a far more important strategical error. Mr. Campbell Stephen, an Independent Labour Party Member for Glasgow, pounced on it in a pungent interruption. Sir John by his motion wished to censure the Prime Minister for interfering unduly in the direction of the war. And here was Sir Roger seconding the motion because the Prime Minister had not sufficiently interfered! One minus one equals nothing.

At the end of the seconder's speech, Churchill and his Ministers could view the debate with some complacency. Their front was not seriously dented and, whatever else might be said of them, their leading critics were not of the stuff from which alternative governments are made.

A few minutes later, the dialectical battle had swung against the Government. In his opening sentences, its first speaker, Mr. Oliver Lyttelton, Minister of Production, annoyed the House by suggesting that it would have been better to have no motion of censure at all. For this he was sharply pulled up by a Conservative Member, Sir Herbert Williams, who pointed out that, in fact, the Government had come into existence as the result of a motion of censure.

The unfortunate Minister went on to irritate his audience still further by declining, in spite of protests, to give way to Mr. Richard Stokes, a respected Labour Member with a formidable knowledge of tank production problems. He bored doggedly on, harried by interrupters. One of these drew the Deputy Speaker's attention to the apparent truth that Mr. Lyttelton was breaking the Parliamentary rule which forbids the reading of a speech. It would in fact have been quite impossible for him to keep in his memory the vast store of figures relating to tank and gun production in a survey of munitions production, which began with the period immediately before the war!

His argument was that, having lost her initial equipment in the French disaster, Britain was condemned to devote a great deal of her production capacity to replacing the lost weapons which, although they might be obsolescent, could be more quickly provided than improved models. There was, consequently, so much the less industrial effort available for making guns and tanks that could meet the enemy on equal terms. The reasoning, if accepted in all its bearings, could only lead to the most gloomy conclusions. Was there, perhaps, a flaw in the argument?

The House of Commons was too resentful of the Minister's manner, or, it may be, too stupefied by his statistics, to probe his logic. A historical survey, however thorough, was, in any case, no answer to the questions uppermost in men's minds: why had the Eighth Army been defeated? Why had Tobruk fallen? And where did the fault lie: in the desert, in Cairo or in Downing Street?

Mr. Lyttelton's answer seemed to be that no individual was to blame for the inferiority in weapons and that some tactical mishap might have occurred in the desert although, as the fighting was still going on, it was hard to be sure. It was not an answer likely to satisfy a jury thirsty for dismissals, impeachments and blood.

When Mr. Lyttelton sat down, badgered to the end, flustered and visibly perspiring, he whispered to his neighbour, Anthony Eden: "I don't know if this is your idea of fun but it's not mine." He had not satisfied—in truth, he had merely stimulated—the reasonable curiosity of the House on these matters. It was a pity, however, that he had lost his audience, for he had first-hand knowledge of the desert fighting. Indeed, he caught its essence in graphic sentences: "An armoured battle in the desert raises a great dust, and movements are very quick. In five or ten minutes the whole direction of the battle changes."

Five speeches further on—speeches which had revealed little beyond the divided minds among members about the convenience of the motion and the proper target for criticism—Flight-Lieutenant Boothby fulfilled his promise, given to the Prime Minister a few hours earlier. As he thought Churchill and his administration should stay in power, it was a waste of time to argue about the machinery of government at the summit. The only criticism of the Government was not that they had failed to do enough but that they had attempted to do too much with the material at their disposal. Boothby went on to speak severely about the slowness with which intelligence crawled through service channels, about the failure to detach heavy bombers to the destruction of North African ports in German hands. But the weight of his advocacy was overwhelmingly on the Government's side. When Boothby sat down, the Prime Minister left the House.

The debate burned on into the summer night, like a sulky fire, now murkily smoking, at moments flaring up into an angry flame.

There was assuredly no lack of fire about the speech of Earl Winterton, an independent-minded Conservative Member, who followed Boothby and brushed aside his suggestion that the preceding Government, Chamberlain's, was responsible for most of the trouble.

Who had controlled the Norwegian operation? "Churchill, then First Lord of the Admiralty. After a series of disasters beyond anything in the First World War, was it to be said that the Prime Minister was the only man who could win the war? The *Führer* is always right."

Never, during thirty-seven years in the House, had he seen such attempts to absolve a Prime Minister from ministerial responsibility. If the disasters went on, Churchill ought to go to his colleagues and offer to serve under one of them, say as Foreign Secretary. At this point in Lord Winterton's speech, the Prime Minister returned to the Chamber. Shouts went up: "Tell him again." There was no need to do so, said Winterton: "if this state of affairs goes on, the country will tell him."

Different aspects of popular feeling were reflected as the debate uncoiled. Was it right to give encouragement to the enemy by a direct challenge to the Prime Minister? Did the weary men defending Tobruk stop to criticize the Prime Minister's direction of the war? No war has been won by inquests but, on the other hand, wars have been lost because the lessons taught by mistakes have been neglected.

Commander Sir Archibald Southby, a naval officer and a Tory who sat for Epsom, attacked naval strategy. He rubbed in the fact that Britain was now reaping in the Mediterranean the fruits of the loss of Singapore and the two capital ships off Malaya. The Prime Minister had met the leaders of the American Congress on 24 June. He had told them, as Mr. Samuel Rayburn, Speaker of the House of Representatives, had reported, that Egypt was in no danger. Surely that had been wide of the mark.

Passing on to speak of the equipment with which the British Army was meeting its enemies, Sir Archibald said it fell short in quality, not in quantity. Too much attention was being paid to the rising curve of production; too little to the quality of what was being produced.

Mr. John McGovern rose after the debate had gone on for eleven and a half hours to report to the House that there was consternation and anger in the country. The Government would not last for a week without the protection it received from Labour Members in the Cabinet, the people who overthrew the Chamberlain Government after the comparatively small reverse in Norway. Now the people were getting tired of the orthodox political parties and there was a throw-up of independent candidates in by-elections. He foresaw a development of the new political organism which Lord Beaverbrook was reported to be financing. True or not? He did not know. But where there is smoke, there is fire. There was going to be a first-class political upheaval and the Government could not last another six months.

Eight speeches later, the debate stumbled to a halt. It had probed this way and that, into leadership, tactics, lack of dive-bombers, production, design, the Prime Minister's dictatorial tendencies, his emotionalism, his lack of foresight etc. It had been told that, at such a critical moment of the war, it ought not to probe at all.

The great enquiry at last exhausted its authors. There were fewer than forty members in the Chamber when someone called for a count. It was twenty minutes to three.

The old chess-room of the House of Commons had been turned into a bar open to M.P.s and members of the press. There, Sir Herbert Williams, a Conservative member of the anti-Churchill faction, remarked gleefully to a porter of his acquaintance:

"We've got the old bugger now!"

But the Government, although damaged by the critics' salvoes, was still afloat at the end of the long day.

The big guns had still to fire.

In the House of Lords that afternoon, a parallel battle had been fought. Lord Beaverbrook, from the front Opposition bench, had defended the Government from the attack launched against it by Lord Addison on a motion, "to call attention to the conduct of the war", which although milder than the censure motion in the Commons, had much the same meaning. For Addison's conclusion was that the Prime Minister had not time to be

Minister of Defence as well. Wavell should be brought home and given the job.

Beaverbrook opened nervously but warmed quickly to his theme, He addressed himself to the production and quality of the weapons at the disposal of the Army. Our 3·7-inch gun was better than the German 88-mm. (The question might be asked, Why was it not used against the German tanks?)

We had more guns and tanks in Libya than the Germans and the Italians put together. Although our tanks did not carry the punch of the Germans, we had some American tanks that could hit even harder. In speed of the tanks there was a rough balance between the two armies; in armour it favoured the British. Only in gunpower, in the six-pounders, he maintained, did the enemy enjoy a real advantage. And we should have had the six-pounders if we had possessed the tanks to carry them.

Beaverbrook's speech, now confident and forceful, was that of a man who had mastered his brief. It was rapid, well-organized, impressively studded with figures; where it explained defects in the situation, the explanations were convincing.

Turning from weapons to leadership, he asked if that was where the trouble lay? It was too early to criticize. Certainly the Government did not interfere with the choice of officers by Auchinleck ("a fine man") nor was the Tobruk disaster due to interference from London. "My experience is that the Prime Minister does everything possible to persuade generals and others to take their full measure of responsibility."

It was a curiously phrased sentence. What kind of general was it that needed to be persuaded to take responsibility? Unless, of course, the Prime Minister had been persuading soldiers to courses of action against their own judgment? That was precisely the burden of many

murmurs against Churchill heard in the military clubs in
Whitehall and elsewhere. But in the warmth of the debate,
the puzzling phrase passed unnoticed.

Beaverbrook concluded by arguing that the final responsibility for strategy must rest on the Prime Minister,
whether he was Defence Minister or not.

It had been a powerful and authoritative defence of the
Government, the more effective as coming from a man
whom rumour suspected of designs on the throne. Supply
of arms, quality of weapons, generalship, and the control
of the war at the summit—all had been examined. Three
of the suspects had been found not guilty. One—generalship—had been put back for further consideration. If
there were any criticism of this brilliant intervention it
was simply that the speaker's scythe had cut down too
many of the thistles of doubt. Had not Lord Beaverbrook
proved too much?

The leading article in *The Times* next morning thought
so. The argument, said the writer, would have been more
convincing had it not been tested by the facts of the battle.
The writer recalled the French surgeon who, when asked
whether the operation succeeded, replied: "Assez bien. Il
est mort, mais il est mort guéri."


Apart from exhibiting the querulous mediocrity of most
of the speakers, the first day's debate in the House of
Commons had done little except to illustrate the weakness
of Parliamentary discussion in wartime as a tool of in-
quiry. The second day opened like a thunderclap with a
speech of dazzling quality by Aneurin Bevan. Here was
impetus of attack, sustained energy of argument, shape
and elegance! Here was a speech worthy of a high national
occasion!

The son of the Welsh valleys and the son of Blenheim

differed in their styles of oratory. Bevan was the more natural speaker of the two; indeed, there had been no public speaker of his quality since Lloyd George. Churchill's oratory was a literary exercise, the product of long preparation and three centuries of British history; a conscious, studied work. But, in some other respects, the two men were not so unlike, each self-taught, each drunk with the learning he had laboriously acquired, each a voluble, dominating conversationalist; at times, an explosive one.

In Bevan, the nature of the man was more generous than his creed. Indeed, on the sole occasion when he was nonplussed in Parliamentary debate—by a woman—it was by an accusation of meanness. And this was lethal because not only was it true, but it charged him with a betrayal of his own essence, which was sweet and poetic. In Bevan, the warmth of the man worked in a coarse grain. In Churchill, a touch of the puritan was present, refining a being that was robust and baroque. The two men disliked one another. Bevan envied Churchill, perhaps because he realized that the older man's rhetorical talent was, in those years, working with the grain of history. On that July night in 1942, Bevan could feel that for once history and his talent were moving in unison.

The Prime Minister had elected to close the debate. Bevan said he should have opened it. The House should be put in possession of the facts. How else could it examine them? By winding up the debate, the Prime Minister had made certain of winning it. The trouble was that he won debate after debate, and lost battle after battle.

Three things were wrong: the main strategy of the war was wrong; the wrong weapons had been produced; and the weapons were being managed by men who had not studied their use. As he understood it, strategy dictates the weapon and tactics dictates it use.

From the start, the war had been misconceived and by

nobody more than Mr. Churchill, who more than anyone was responsible for Britain's lack of transport aircraft
and dive-bombers.

Strategy was wrong because the Prime Minister seemed
to think of war in terms of a medieval tourney. And since
the War Cabinet was composed of ministers overburdened, for the most part, with departmental duties, all the
Prime Minister's natural weaknesses were exaggerated.

He had qualities of greatness, but he had too much to
do and no colleague to whom he could delegate anything
concerning the central direction of the war. He had, too, a
dangerous gift of expression, often mistaking verbal feli-
cities for verbal inspiration.

The House should, for Heaven's sake, put the Prime
Minister under the clamp of strong men with no departmental interests. Everyone knew that this was the right
thing to do. Why did the House of Commons not exert its
dignity and force the Prime Minister to do it?

Under the War Cabinet, he suggested, there should be a
central staff presided over by one man who would be ulti-
mately responsible for central strategy. He agreed that
the Prime Minister should not have a Minister of Defence.
The Prime Minister could not delegate responsibility for
the war to anyone else. But he could have around him a
number of Ministers to assist him in that matter.

In a prolonged flight of patriotic passion Bevan, spokesman at that moment of a proud, humiliated people,
brought his speech to a close. When he sat down, a Scottish Tory, Walter Elliot, delivered judgment. "We have at
last," he declared, "heard the authentic voice of a vote of
censure."

But was it? Did the argument match the eloquence?
What, in fact, had Bevan finally said?

He had conceded that Churchill must remain Prime
Minister, with the ultimate, inescapable responsibility for

the war, but demanded that he be surrounded and assisted in the supreme direction of the war by a group of Ministers untrammelled by the care of departments of state. But was not a vote of censure a demand for a change at the summit? If it succeeded, would it not be followed inevitably by the resignation of the Prime Minister?

In the strange circumstances of July 1942, the normal rules and procedures of Parliament were hardly relevant. A vote of censure implied an organized opposition, an alternative Government waiting in the wings. Nothing of the kind existed. Even this single foray against Churchill and his methods had turned out to be a confused affair, ill-organized, disunited. The Government engrossed most of the political talent of all three parties. Were it to fall, its successor would of necessity be built mainly out of the same bricks. Few indeed were the men of ministerial quality in the wilderness.

One of them was Leslie Hore-Belisha, former Minister of War, dismissed in 1940, as a victim of a military cabal and, out of office, not to be comforted. Soon after his dismissal, the weekly review *Truth* had published two articles about his adventures in the City ten years earlier. In these it was recalled that Belisha had been director of some companies in which their investors had lost a great deal of money. Some of Belisha's party colleagues said at the time that he would have no more influence with them until he brought a libel action against *Truth*. This he never did. But his exile from office gnawed at his soul. "What are you worrying about?" said Shinwell to him one day. "There is plenty of fun in opposition." "It is all right for you," said Belisha gloomily, "you have a following in the country."

Belisha rose to support the motion of censure. The time for dialectics had passed, he said; now debate must lead to a conclusion. Defeats had occurred because of false appreciations, consistent misjudgments. There had been a mistake over Greece, failure to understand the significance of Rommel's arrival in Africa, boastful claims about what the army was doing—or was about to do—in Libya.

The armament available to the generals was progressively described as ample, of equal quality to the enemy's, of superior quality! When rout followed where victory had been predicted, what inference was drawn? That the generals were to blame! This was ungenerous—as it was unworthy to blame the Army and contemptible to blame the Government's predecessors.

There could be no doubt at whom this stream of criticism was aimed. Churchill had been the vainglorious spokesman, given to disparaging the nerve and power of the enemy and prone to celebrating victories before they were won.

How, asked Belisha, could one place reliance on judgments that had so repeatedly turned out to be misguided? "We are concerned less with the fate of the Government than with the fate of the country. It is not by over-confidence, not by boasting or arrogance or rhetoric that we shall win this war. It is by a humble devotion to our task with the knowledge that, if we fail, a thousand years of British history are over." Belisha had made a powerful contribution to the case against the Government. If it lacked the ultimate, lethal force of attack, this was because many of the listeners believed that Belisha's support for Churchill could be won, with a Ministry.

The long debate had reached its climax.

To the accompaniment of a long roll of cheering, the Prime Minister rose in his place on the front bench. The Chamber was crowded, more crowded even than for that earlier debate after Singapore had fallen. Three officer

M.P.s sat or sprawled on the floor; behind them an M.P. in private's uniform beside a colonel in the red tabs of the staff. Prince Bernhard of the Netherlands listened from above. The doors of the crowded peers' gallery were open so that peers unable to gain admittance could hear from the passage outside.

Churchill began talking quietly, without emotion, in that half-conversational manner in which Parliamentary speeches should open and in which they sometimes end. Yet it was not possible for a trained ear to miss the heightened, yet reined-in, emotion in the melodious growling voice. It came in part from the speaker, in part from the occasion, in part from the audience.

This was the Commons, the august assembly, the culmination of a long, wavering but unbroken tradition of incomparable majesty. He who grumbled out those first sentences of his reply to the debate was more aware of its grandeur than most men—the ultimate tribunal with the power to be callous or stupid, to dismiss, to condemn without appeal. He knew. Now the whips were on his side as once—twice—how often?—they had worked against him. But the whips who could and would prevent his defeat in the lobbies had no power over an entity less tangible than votes which he, Churchill, acknowledged—the "feeling of the House"—the consensus of five or six hundred men. Over that hovering spirit he must prevail. He approached the prickly animal with the infinite precautions of one who had felt its claws.

The first strokes of brush on canvas were tentative; yet it was soon clear that the master had embarked on another of his vast landscapes of the war, majestic in its sweep and scale but not neglecting in all its skilfully disposed confusion the shrewdness of advocacy.

They were in the presence, he said, of a recession of their hopes and prospects in the Middle East and in the

Mediterranean unequalled since the fall of France. If
there were any would-be profiteers of disaster who felt
able to paint the picture in darker colours, they were
certainly at liberty to do so!

Dealing lightly with one of the charges against him, he
said of course it was absolutely impossible to fight battles
from Westminster or Whitehall. The less one interfered
the better. This sentence might have brought a smile to
the face of commanders who had been harassed by
Churchill's non-interference.

The logistics of the war in the desert were obviously
against us. It needed four months to send a weapon
round the Cape and perhaps a week or even less to send it
across the Mediterranean. Thus it might be that we were
relatively no better off in the middle of May than in
March or April—100,000 against 90,000 of the enemy (of
whom 50,000 were Germans); a superiority in number of
tanks of seven to five, and of guns of eight to five. One
might say that in this extraordinary situation the forces
assembled on both sides represented a war effort which in
other theatres would have amounted to three or four times
their numbers.

This was, of course, true, although it was also true that
to bring a German to the African battlefield cost a much
smaller effort than was needed to put an Englishman
there. It was an inexorable handicap which, from beginning to end, weighed on the desert operation.

Conscious of the drama in the House, the Prime
Minister was with half of his mind and most of his imagination engaged on a more desperate struggle, unresolved,
the battle in Africa which was still being fought. He described its course—the hopeful opening, the fatal night of
13 June when we had 300 tanks in the morning, of which
by nightfall only seventy remained, excluding the light
Stuarts.

Had there been any failure by the Government to sustain that front? In the last two years 950,000 men, 4,500 tanks, 6,000 aircraft and 5,000 guns had gone to the Middle East. As for quality, he agreed with Aneurin Bevan that the House should read Lord Beaverbrook's "masterly, intricate and authoritative" statement of the facts.

Turning with a show of anger on his critics, some of whom, like Bevan, had got under his guard, he defended himself against the charge of undue optimism, denying for example that he had ever said that Singapore would hold out. "What a fool and knave I should have been to say that it would fall!"

At the end came flattery for the House, to whom he owed much. It must be a steady, stabilizing factor in the State and not an instrument by which the disaffected sections of the press could attempt to promote one crisis after another. Governments, resting on democratic institutions, should be able to act and dare, the servants of the Crown must not be harassed by nagging and snarling. Sober and constructive criticism had its high virtue, but the duty of the House of Commons was to sustain the Government or to change the Government. If it could not change it, it should sustain it.

"I am your servant, and you have the right to dismiss me when you please. What you have not the right to do is to ask me to bear responsibilities without the power of effective action."

He closed with a passage of ponderous irony. Sir John Wardlaw-Milne had proposed that some military figure or other unnamed personage should have complete control of the armed forces, be Chief of the Chiefs of Staff, that he should always be ready to resign if he did not get all he wanted and finally should find an appendage in the Prime Minister to make the necessary explanations, excuses and apologies to Parliament. "I shall take no part in such a system," said Churchill.

It was time to vote.

The debate had been mismanaged from the start. In the first few minutes, as we have seen, Sir John Wardlaw-Milne had made a blunder so monumental that the House had exploded in a derision from which it did not completely recover all through the first day. Worse, Sir John and Sir Roger, proposer and seconder, had marched into battle under different flags and launched their attacks in opposite directions. In the ranks of the Government's critics were too many disappointed and inconsolable politicians, men like Clement Davies who believed he had been one of the main architects of Chamberlain's downfall and was correspondingly bitter at being denied a place in Churchill's Cabinet.

Every kind of subordinate issue—tank types, gun types, dive-bombers, problems of design and question of supply—had been explored, or rather peered at with the flickering candles of half-knowledge. All these were departmental matters. But this was a debate about the central conduct of the war, held in the shadow of successive disasters. The issue was, not whether the Army wanted dive-bombers, but whether the grand strategy of the war was being shaped and carried out with sufficient deliberation. The weight of evidence was against such a belief. The evidence of defeat. By failing to keep discussion firmly aimed at that target, the House of Commons fell short of its duty. "From the first words of Sir John Wardlaw-Milne to the last words of Mr. Churchill," said the *Evening News*, "one looks in vain for anything that throws a clear light on the cause of the Libyan defeat."

It may be admitted that the formula of a motion of censure was ill chosen for such an occasion: it attacked a man while what was wanted was to make a reasoned case for a change in the system—a change which had illustrious precedent in Lloyd George's War Cabinet. Only by rare flashes did this purpose appear amidst the welter of argument.

As it was, Churchill had an easy task in answering the debate. His reply was that of a man who could speak with knowledge where others could only guess at the facts. It was a tissue of truths and half-truths, impressively studded with figures. His counter-attacks on the critics had a stinging glee which theirs had lacked.

The reply was good; too good. His basic argument was that Parliament must sustain him or dismiss him. It had no other duty. But this was arrogant nonsense. It was not Churchill's right to insist that the war must be conducted in his way. It was Parliament's duty to maintain a steady and, if possible, well-informed supervision over the running of the machine—and to order changes in design where these seemed necessary. There was reason to think them necessary then.

The war *was* going badly. Churchill *was* overburdened. He did interfere in too many things. He insisted on having a monopoly of strategy and he told Parliament that he would not serve as Prime Minister on any other terms. And this was something he had no right to do. But he did it. With remarkable audacity and spirit, he stood among the ruins of his policy—Singapore lost, Tobruk gone, Egypt in danger, India threatened—and demanded that Parliament grant him a renewal of the lease on his quasi-dictatorship. He was an extraordinary man.

But it was time to vote.


By the tally in the division lobbies, 476 members voted with the Government (among them Mr. Driberg, the newly elected independent Member for Maldon) and twenty-five against. It was estimated that forty members who were in the House abstained from voting. Twelve of them were Conservatives. When the result of the voting was announced, a great cheer went up. Mr. Churchill exchanged smiles with his family in the gallery, gave the V-sign and left the Chamber.

## CHAPTER XIV
# "Mr. Churchill's Privy Council"

*Success, like charity, covers a multitude of sins.*
—Mahan

ON THE DAY AFTER THE DEBATE in London, General Auchinleck sent a signal to the Eighth Army in the Desert: "Well done, everybody. A very good day. Stick to it." Rommel's advance on the Nile had been halted.

A fortnight later, in what has been called the First Battle of El Alamein, the Afrika Korps was decisively repulsed. Cruelly singling out the Italians for attention, Auchinleck beat the spirit out of his opponents. The ladies of Alexandria would sigh in vain for their German lovers. As the German Chief of Staff, General Bayerlein, wrote, "When Rommel lost Tel el Eisa and Ruweisat, he and all of us knew we were lost".

Forbidden by the *Führer* to retreat, Rommel was left at the end of an unconscionably long line of communications while the army opposite him was reinforced by the equivalent of two new armoured divisions equipped with modern tanks and—at last—a hundred self-propelled guns. There were also going to be two fresh infantry divisions. Whoever met Rommel next time would do so on vastly more favourable terms.

But, whoever it was, it was not going to be Sir Claude Auchinleck, victor of the First Battle of El Alamein.* On 3

* The earliest mention of the name seems to be an entry in Major-General Dorman-Smith's diary for 1 July: "Battle of El Alamein."

August, the Prime Minister arrived in Cairo; three days later, he decided Auchinleck must go. General Alexander would take his place in Cairo, while in the desert General Montgomery would reign—or rather would rule! The latter faced his new job with spry self-confidence: "I've never taken on a Field-Marshal before," he said.

In the crisis that existed, the removal of Auchinleck was no doubt a harsh but wise decision: a drastic reconstruction of the high command was needed if the shaken morale of the Eighth Army was to be restored. But the change had a further implication: by removing Auchinleck, the Prime Minister was in effect fixing on him the responsibility for the fall of Tobruk. This had been only a major incident in a long fluctuating battle. More important was the command and the spirit of the Army.

The disaster had provided the impetus for the attack on Churchill in the House of Commons. Responsibility for it was a main and legitimate matter for Parliamentary enquiry. Sir John Wardlaw-Milne had asked whether the orders to hold—and then to surrender—Tobruk were given in London, Washington, Cairo or the desert. And Churchill had replied with derision: did Sir John really imagine that he, Churchill, sent from Washington an order to capitulate? The decision was taken by the commander in the field.

The question and the answer show the limitation of Parliamentary discussion as an instrument for ascertaining the truth about complex issues, especially in war-time. Neither the Prime Minister nor the Chief of the Imperial General Staff had "ordered" Tobruk to be held. That was certain. But the Prime Minister had sent Auchinleck that telegram of 14 June, "Presume there is no question in any case of giving up Tobruk" . . .

This was moral pressure, stern and peremptory, exerted from the summit. It arrived at a moment when Auchinleck and General Ritchie, Commander of the Eighth

Army, were grappling with the problem of the battle in the desert of which Tobruk was only one aspect. Ritchie had offered his chief the choice between risking a siege of Tobruk and evacuating the "fortress" so that the whole army could be pulled back to the Egyptian frontier, eighty miles to the east. Auchinleck had decided that Tobruk could be held, although the enemy must not be allowed to invest it.

Ritchie, the man on the spot, felt in his bones that he could not hold Tobruk as part of a line of defence. He was ordered to do just that. Another telegram came from Churchill accepting Auchinleck's "assurance" that he had no intention of giving up Tobruk. Ritchie found himself told to do something he knew could not be done. And Auchinleck found himself drawn into a course of action which he had decided (19 January, 1942) should never be undertaken. So Tobruk was isolated; and so Tobruk was lost.

This significant incident illustrates in summary the essential features of the Churchill system:

(1) The soldier's instinct to obey an order—a factor which the Prime Minister could, and did, exploit.

(2) A stream of admonitory and minatory messages which fell short of orders. These may, at times, have been needless. At times, they may have been exasperating. But how else can a national leader ensure that there is no failure of resource, energy or resolution?

(3) Ignorance in London of the local situation. This did not prevent the sending of telegrams, but could— if things went wrong—become a ground for asserting that the telegrams had never been orders. "We did not, however, know the conditions prevailing in Tobruk," wrote Churchill later. "It was inconceivvable that the already well-proved fortifications of

Tobruk should not have been maintained in the highest efficiency."

(4) Failure by Cairo to paint the situation in the grim colours of reality. Had this been done, it would certainly have provoked an explosion in Downing Street. It might have led to the dismissal of Auchinleck, who was dismissed anyhow a few weeks later, but it would have pierced the clouds of self-deception in which the Prime Minister was apt to wrap himself. Perhaps Cairo did not itself know the full truth about "the fortress of Tobruk". After all, in the middle of a great battle, pictures are rarely clear, in the field, at the base or in the distant Cabinet room.

(5) A tendency for Churchill's strategical supervision to grow by way of distrust of his soldiers into an interference with their conduct of a battle.

The disease seems to have been endemic among the civilian chieftains of the nations at war. "I had the impression," writes Marshal Zhukov, "that the military were invited to the Kremlin not in order to discuss the counter-offensive but simply because Stalin wanted to 'prod them', as he often used to say."[1]

The debate in the House of Commons had been concerned with these grave matters. The vote had given the Prime Minister an extension of his system. But the extension amounted to no more than an admission that, where nobody knew what was wrong, nobody could convincingly put forward a remedy. Parliament had been proved a dog whose bark was stronger than its scent.

The shrewdest comment on Middle East strategy had come from Churchill, its author, when he told the House that four (or six) months were needed to carry men and weapons from Britain to the desert—and that he had sent 950,000 men there. It seemed that this was hardly the more economical use of resources which sea-power was supposed to confer. But it was necessary to build up the Middle East as a great base, political as well as military—almost a second United Kingdom. For this reason, a great many men must be sent there.

Besides, the Middle East *had* been an area where Britain could fight a limited war against a superior adversary. After Rommel had established himself in Libya, that situation was certainly altered to Britain's disadvantage. But this was a question which could not be decided on purely military grounds. The desert was, during long grey months of war, the only theatre where British troops were at grips with the enemy. The alternative to fighting there was total idleness, which was morally and psychologically impossible. This was a factor which generals could, perhaps, ignore, but which could not be absent for a minute from the Prime Minister's mind. As General George Marshall put it, "The great lesson I learned in 1942 was that in war politicians have to do *something* important every year".[2] Churchill had learned the lesson, if he needed to learn it, before 1942. In war, nations as well as politicians must "do something important every year".

The significance of Churchill's admission about the influence of the time-lag on the desert war was lost in the House during the final minutes of the debate.

In the high summer of 1942, the beam of public interest in Britain swung away from Libya. "Somewhere on the sweeping plains between two Russian rivers, the fate of this planet is being decided. The British people ask: Must we stand aside as spectators at Armageddon?"[3] The statement was dramatic but hardly exaggerated. The fate of the planet, or at least the shape, duration and maybe outcome of the war in which the planet was engulfed, turned upon military developments in southern Russia which were now mounting towards a tremendous crisis.

While the British people "stood aside", the German armies pressed on eastwards against what seemed to be a faltering Russian resistance. On 20 July, Hitler told his Chief of Staff, Colonel-General Halder: "The Russian is finished." Halder was inclined to agree. "It looks like it."

By 23 August, the Fourteenth Panzer Corps had reached the banks of the Volga on the northern outskirts of Stalingrad. It seemed that the fall of this key industrial city was imminent. Certainly the culmination of the Russian campaign was at hand. In rubble, sewers, cellars, amid the concrete ruins of factories and the brick heaps that had been workers' flats, the terrible and extraordinary battle of Stalingrad was about to begin.

For weeks and months a pall of smoke hung over the Volga and, in imagination, came to fill the autumn sky for millions of people in Britain who knew by instinct that, if Stalin's city fell, some frightening new phase in the war would open; and who, as time passed, began to cherish the hope, at first desperate and then stronger, that somehow, by some miracle of improvisation and fanaticism, in those last few yards of shattered streets west of the Volga, Stalingrad would hold out. Gripped by this drama, torn between such fears and such hopes, public, newspapers and Parliament broke out afresh in impatience over the apparent inadequacy of the part Britain was playing in the crisis. "A supreme Allied Council of War, if we had one, would see in Stalingrad the centre of world-wide strategy."[4]

The Dieppe raid on 19 August had raised for a moment the spirits of those who thought that it might be a precursor, perhaps even the beginning, of the Second Front. Its failure, seeping through to public awareness in the last days of August, brought about a new wave of gloom and exasperation

The appalling story of the Anglo-American Arctic convoy PQ17, which sailed from Iceland on 17 June and was destroyed—twenty-three vessels sunk out of thirty-four—in the first weeks of July, might have made people realize the sacrifices Russia's allies were making in efforts to help her. But the news of this tragic incident was shrouded by secrecy and leaked out only through the terrifying stories spread by survivors.

The general frustration was fully shared in Parliament. But, after the defeat of the attempt to impose its will—or rather, its vague sense that some change ought to come—on the Prime Minister, the House of Commons was irritable, discontented, mutinous rather than rebellious.

On 9 September, Churchill conducted one of his surveys of the war. The canvas was emptier than usual, the painting sketchier. The speech was a failure. Members began to drift out while it was still in progress. When it ended, the Chamber was all but empty. Sixteen Members were left to hear Arthur Greenwood, "Leader of the Opposition". The debate died. One member said: "This is a complete farce. There must be three hundred Members in the precincts."

To an ill-judged rebuke from Sir Stafford Cripps ("We cannot conduct Parliamentary business with dignity unless Members are prepared to pay greater attention to their duties") the House reacted with ill-humour. In any important debate, the Members were in a quandary, as Vernon Bartlett, M.P. for Bridgwater, pointed out:[5] they could not prepare their speeches until the Prime Minister had finished speaking and then they must retire to revise their notes. "Don't accuse us in one breath of wasting time in talk and in the next of failing in our duties if we keep silent."

The incident suggested that Churchill had momentarily

lost the ear of the House and that Cripps was riding the Members on too tight a rein.

But the real trouble lay deeper. A system of war-time government had been created which concentrated power in a single person without providing automatic checks on the use of that power. Normal methods of opposition were stifled under the coalition. Public opinion was frustrated by the agreement between the party machines, and criticism by the need for secrecy. The Prime Minister was apt to view any request to re-examine his policy as mere factious opposition. "There is no coherent relation between Mr. Churchill and Parliament or between Mr. Churchill and the general public. The first has become his privy council, the second his unseen audience. He is responsible only to himself and to the muse of history."[6]

Would the progressive enfeeblement of Parliament be arrested if the party truce were ended? Could the breach between Government and nation be healed by means of a general election? A Clydeside Socialist, George Buchanan, dismissed the notion as chimerical: "The Churchill ticket would dominate; reason and argument would be gone. Not a single candidate would win an election against the Prime Minister."

Should Churchill find it necessary, in some emergency, to seek public support over the head of the House, then, thought Robert Bootbhy, there would be a general election. But not otherwise.

Would a general election, whatever its outcome, have brought about any real change in the British political system? It may be doubted. On the whole, it seems more likely that, in the circumstances of war, the relative positions of Parliament, Cabinet and Prime Minister which were charted in 1942 represented a stage in the adjustment of British democracy to modern conditions.

Mr. R. H. S. Crossman, writing twenty years after these

events,[7] observed how the British people willingly exchanged their democratic constitution for a centralized autocracy in order to meet the challenge of total war. He adds: "What is not so often noticed is the extent to which the institutions and the behaviour of voluntary totalitarianism have been retained since 1945." What vestige of the war-time system would remain when peace returned was, however, a question that nobody posed in 1942. What was clear was that Parliament was necessarily handicapped and the Government abnormally invulnerable.

This, at least, was unlikely to be changed by a general election, should one be held in an emergency which, that autumn, was a prospect only too real and immediate. Russian resistance at Stalingrad, every day more irrational, desperate and heroic, might collapse before Britain had engaged the enemy with the full weight of her forces. In that case there would indeed be a political crisis.

On 9 September, Aneurin Bevan had launched a cruel arrow at Churchill's strategy. The Italians, he said, could afford to send more troops to Russia than they had in Egypt.[8] "Hitler is luckier in his allies than Stalin is." Here was Stalingrad besieged and almost fallen, with only forty-five German divisions in the West. "I say that this year, fought with imagination and courage, the Germans could have been beaten." Bevan's comment might be unfair but, if defeat came to Stalingrad, the shaft might fester quickly in the Government's flesh.

Another voice, which the muse of history may have heard with a sardonic smile, summoned the nation from sloth. Sir Samuel Hoare, once a Minister in Chamberlain's administration, a champion of appeasement and a trafficker with Laval over Abyssinia, paid England a visit from his Embassy in Madrid. And one day, a fortnight after Aneurin Bevan's speech, Hoare addressed a nation which seemed to be "permanently settled down to a war dispensation". A greater sense of urgency was needed, lest victory should not be won before Europe had expired through starvation and exhaustion. "Speed, speed, speed. I repeat the cry of suffering Europe."

About the same time, the Prime Minister was receiving from a new quarter advice on how to organize at the summit of affairs an efficient machine to conduct the war to victory. Since his mission to India had ended in disappointment, Sir Stafford Cripps had "lost touch" with the House of Commons and with the puritanical fringes of the Left who were anxious, so they said, for Britain to imitate the sacrificial exertions of Russia. Gone were the days when he appeared, a stern young prophet, fresh from the snows of Russia. In the month of June, a Socialist journalist[9] complained that Cripps had spoken to a Fabian Society luncheon like a *Daily Telegraph* leading article. "I wept bitter tears both for Sir Stafford and for the public whose clamour forced him into the War Cabinet." By October, Claud Cockburn, writing in *The Week*, a journal whose influence was wider than its sales might suggest, spoke with greater cruelty of one who had been "a sort of *éminence beige* of the War Cabinet but is now chiefly the subject of speculation as to just when he will next decide not to resign on a matter of principle".

The inference that Cripps was unhappy in his position was probably justified. In the beginning of October he told Eden that he had reached the parting of the ways with Churchill, on whom he had urged—it was the Hankey plan, the Bevan plan, the plan of all the men who believed that a change in the machinery of control would work a miracle—a War Cabinet of Ministers without departments to worry about who would act as a central thinking and planning instrument. Lacking such a body, problems of strategy were conceived hurriedly, without sufficient information and often in isolation.

To these proposals the Prime Minister listened with some astonishment. They had an air of familiarity. They were, after all, substantially the same as those espoused by the more coherent of his critics in the debate of censure. They had been considered by Parliament and, one must assume, decisively rejected.

Churchill's patience was tried still further by the gloomy reports his Leader of the House simultaneously brought him bearing on the state of national morale. The Prime Minister was well posted on topics of this kind through his admirable Minister of Information and loyal friend, Brendan Bracken. He was disposed to think that the account Cripps brought him was some distillation of the too-lucid thinking and too-anxious expectations which, he had no doubt, prevailed among the left-wing intellectuals with whom Cripps might be expected to consort.

The autumn of 1942, with a new battle preparing in one corner of Africa and a vast new invasion about to be launched in another, was not a time to speak to the Prime Minister of faltering nerve among the public. However, Cripps pressed his criticisms, his proposals and his sense of frustration to the point of resigning. On the entreaty of Eden and others, his resignation was withheld until the new phase in the African war should be launched. As Churchill had said to Stalin one evening in Moscow after speaking with some enthusiasm of Cripps's virtues, "The trouble is, his chest is a cage in which two squirrels are at war, his conscience and his career."[10]

Criticism of the Government muttered on in the press and in Parliament. The "Second Front" was a slogan for factory walls, occasional leading articles in the *Daily Express* and a topic for querulous comment by the Russian Ambassador, Maisky, who irritated the Foreign Office by telling American journalists that the American Government wished to launch the invasion of Europe but

that the British hung back. But in truth some of the wind
had gone out of those once swelling sails of propaganda.

In the middle of August Churchill had journeyed
to Moscow and confronted Stalin in Moscow. He had
returned convinced that his visit had been a success (an
opinion with which not everyone agreed) and that Stalingrad would be held (of which Brooke, Chief of the Imperial General Staff, was reported to be less confident).

The arch-champion of the Second Front himself, Lord
Beaverbrook, having done more than his share to save the
Government during the critical first day of the censure
debate, having paid the debt of friendship and enjoyed
again the pleasures of power without its responsibilities,
had retired to the sidelines. He was by this time completely restored in health. The severe nervous strain of the
Battle of Britain period lay in the past, the damage it had
inflicted was healed. Fretting in idleness, he looked with
something less than satisfaction on the ministry he had
helped to preserve by his speech in the House of Lords.
At times he was tempted to listen to siren voices, above
all the voice of Churchill holding out a glass of brandy
after lunch one day and saying: "It is time you came back
into the Government, Max."

But come back as what? One day it was to go to Cairo,
and preside over the great spring-cleaning that was due in
that theatre. Then it was to be High Commissioner for the
West Indies. This post Beaverbrook would have accepted,
but the Prime Minister withdrew the offer almost as soon
as he made it. Or it was Moscow, and the welcoming
smile of Stalin, who liked Beaverbrook above all the
British. Once it was the War Office, when some injudicious friends of Beaverbrook's had spread the rumour
that he was the War Minister Britain was waiting for.
Embarrassing! For Churchill was only too ready to rid
himself of his Secretary for War, Sir James Grigg, only

too ready to welcome the prodigal back. He offered the post to Beaverbrook, who was put in the position where he must either disown his champions or take the office.

Most glittering offer of all, it was the Washington Embassy, with everything it meant in influence and power on two shores of the Atlantic, with all the appeal it held to his nature, intensely British in loyalty but American— North American—by the boldness and zest of his temperament. Ambassador in Washington? Might he not play, in the months ahead, an almost pro-consular role? If the possibility was visible to Beaverbrook, it was not overlooked by Churchill, whom it did not daunt. To bring his friend back into the circle of government the Prime Minister was ready to carry out an elaborate re-shuffle of offices: Sir John Anderson to be Viceroy of India; Lord Halifax to become Lord President of the Council; thus making room in the Embassy in Washington for Lord Beaverbrook.

Inevitably some rumour of those enticements reached other members of the Government, who heard them with varying degrees of enthusiasm. Ernest Bevin was among those who looked on them with gloom. Meeting Brendan Bracken one day, he accused him of being under the thumb of the "press lords", especially Beaverbrook, whom the Prime Minister evidently meant to bring back into the Government. No good would come of it, Bevin predicted.

The clue to Churchill's anxiety to see Beaverbrook playing a part again in the Government, and to Bevin's dislike of the prospect, may be found in a remark the Canadian made to Sir Charles Wilson: "The Prime Minister, Brendan and I used to meet every evening. We settled most things." A "kitchen Cabinet"? Nothing could be more obnoxious to a devotee of protocol like Bevin—or to a precisian like Cripps.

But, in truth, it was unlikely that any change would be made in the ministry until the grandiose military issues in Africa were resolved one way or another. If all went well, if the enormous preponderance of material behind the British positions in the desert brought a decisive victory over Rommel, then Churchill's authority would be confirmed and his methods of conducting the war would become unassailable. As for Cripps, his position as he wryly acknowledged, would be destroyed. On the other hand, if the British armament in Egypt were once more mishandled and victory were again denied to the Eighth Army, then the political consequences would be far-reaching. The crisis which the censure debate had postponed would return, vastly bigger and more formidable. This time it would overwhelm the Government.

Brendan Bracken called on Sir Charles Wilson on the last day of September and spoke of the effect of a victory by Rommel: "You see, Charles, important changes in the direction of the war would then be inevitable, and Winston will never submit to any curtailment of his powers. If we are beaten in this battle, it's an end of Winston. Is he sleeping all right?"[11]

On the day after this question was put to the doctor, Churchill had the interview with Cripps which upset him so much. And Beaverbrook told Eden of his anxiety about Winston's health: he was "bowed"; not the man he had been.[12]

Bowed he might be, and with good reason, bearing on his shoulders for so long alone a burden which, as every day brought the hour of battle nearer, grew every day more intolerable. It was no wonder that those who worked closely with him—Brooke, Bracken, and others—found that his temper had an edge on it: "Is the Prime Minister all right, Charles? I thought he was going to hit me."[13] The truth was that Churchill knew he had reached the end of the road. If the coming battle in Egypt went against the Eighth Army, he was finished.

The suspense in Downing Street spread through Whitehall and Westminster. The electricity of those late October days crackled into strange rumours.

For example: one of our pilots, flying to Gibraltar, fell into the sea off Cadiz. On his body was a letter to the Governor of Gibraltar telling the whole story of the impending operation in Africa. Somewhere in Africa? But where? Dakar was the favourite candidate. At any rate, the Spaniards had not, it seemed, found the letter. Fortune—or was it M.I.6?—was on our side!

Another story: an officer engaged on staffwork for the operation carried a letter in his pocket containing the secret of the forthcoming invasion. He had posted a private letter in the black-out and the secret document had fallen, unnoticed, to the ground outside the pillar box. There, in the morning, it was found by a charwoman who, not knowing what to do with it, had given it to an aircraftsman of her acquaintance who was about to be given a commission in the R.A.F. Recognizing the importance of the find, he took it to an R.N.R. lieutenant he knew, refusing to let him see it but asking what he ought to do with it. The lieutenant advised him to take it to the Director of Intelligence. Thus, a second time, the Lord was with us.

On 23 October, the long oppressive quiet was broken. In the full moon, a thousand guns opened fire on the German batteries in the desert. Twenty minutes later, the range shortened, so that the barrage fell on the enemy's forward positions. Infantry and tanks began to move. The Battle of El Alamein had opened.

On 6 November, after fourteen days of difficult fighting and unbearable tension, of heavy losses and swaying fortunes, Rommel's army, its armour destroyed, streamed away to the West. General Alexander signalled victory to the Prime Minister who, however, had the prudence to keep the church bells silent for a little longer. Within twenty-four hours, the invasion of North Africa began at Algiers.

A hard and dreadful chapter of the war was over and—to speak of less important matters—Winston Churchill need not fear his critics in the Government, in Parliament, or elsewhere. One of them, one of the most pertinacious and effective, Emanuel Shinwell, rose (as did Sir John Wardlaw-Milne) to the level of the occasion. "It would be churlish, almost to the point of offensiveness," he told the House of Commons, "not to congratulate the Prime Minister on the remarkable success that has attended our army. The Prime Minister has endured with fortitude an incredible succession of setbacks and disappointments. He has not been unduly favoured by fortune. That is all the more reason why those of us who have indulged occasionally in severe criticism of the Government should join in the chorus of praise that has suddenly descended on his head."

While Shinwell was speaking in London, the Russians launched to the north and south of Stalingrad the attacks which brought about the encirclement and eventually the destruction of the German Sixth Army. So, within a few days, the tide of war turned in two continents.

And, so that the glory should be shared among the different arms, in the last hours of the dying year, five British destroyers and two corvettes, under the command of Captain R. St. V. Sherbrooke, v.c., fought a heroic and victorious action in the Arctic. In this they drove off a German force consisting of the pocket-battleship *Lützow*, the cruiser *Hipper* and six destroyers, seeking to destroy a convoy bound for Russia. This brilliant action bore rich and surprising fruits. First the *Führer's* headquarters learned that a red glow in the Arctic twilight had been reported by a U-boat. This was thought to indicate a German success. Later, when the truth became known, Hitler was thrown into one of his storms of rage. He dismissed Grand Admiral Raeder, and ordered that all large German surface craft should be put out of commission and no more should be built.

Thus, in triumph, the terrible year came to an end.

# Epilogue

*If it is a prince who builds his power on the people, one who can command and is a man of courage, who does not despair in adversity . . . and who wins general allegiance by his personal qualities and the institutions he establishes, he will never be let down by the people.*
—Machiavelli, *The Prince*, chapter 9.

THE POLITICAL CAMPAIGN AGAINST CHURCHILL had found its origin in a string of military disasters which brought into question the whole conception of the war, the design on which it should be fought. This overall strategy was a highly personal matter, a privilege, almost a possession, to which the Prime Minister clung with jealous tenacity.

This was *his* war, waged as his impulse, intuition and restless experimental genius might dictate. And his mind, moving in long, unpredictable leaps, was a bewildering phenomenon which at times seemed utterly irrational to the more conventional intellects about him who were apt to mistake brooding silence for inattention, and sudden decision for irresponsibility. Occasionally they wondered whether the dazzling flights of genius were not, after all, mere excursions into fantasy. But Churchill was there, the offspring of an irretrievable calamity for which he had less guilt than most and to which, sharing the sublime folly of his fellow-countrymen, he had refused to surrender.

What could bring down a man whom ruin had raised?

The battleships lost in the Gulf of Siam; Singapore; Tobruk—three times the bell had tolled. And what had the sequel been? The grey men of experience, high priests of traditional wisdom, had come gravely together, not to remove the man but to amend his method. To install a governor on this too impetuous engine. He should be no longer the supreme warlord, scolding the soldiers and frowning over the maps, but, in a council of luminous and unfettered talents, *primus inter pares*. It was another way of saying that Churchill was necessary and dangerous.

When the decisive trial of strength came in July, after the third disaster, the man had insisted on his method, and Parliament had confirmed the man in his office. Then after a long delay and laborious preparations, came victory in the field, relaxation of political tensions and, as it seemed, a complete vindication of Churchill's strategy.

Blunders there might have been along the way, errors and oversights, in Greece, over the battleships, in the manner in which Malaya was reinforced. These were put aside. The desert war, in which every canon of logistics seemed to be stood on its head, had evolved into a wide, two-pronged operation, embracing the whole of the North African coast and drawing in German and Italian troops (including four armoured divisions) until a quarter of a million enemy soldiers were there.

When the last of those soldiers filed into the prisoner-of-war cages in Tunisia and the count of captured enemy guns reached a thousand, Churchill's obstinate attachment to the Africa campaign, rousing a corresponding and disastrous obstinacy in Hitler, had yielded a splendid harvest.

It seemed that those who had cried, "with veiled menaces and less veiled slanders"[1] for a Second Front were discredited, along with those who had protested against the locking up of tonnage to supply the Middle East. "The triumph of the Eighth Army in Egypt was the signal for the opening of a Grand Design beside which the smooth planned pounces of the Nazi machine may yet pale into historical insignificance."

But in the unfolding of the Design, many disappointments and delays came to light. The soft underbelly of the Axis in the Mediterranean, of which Churchill had spoken so ardently to Stalin, would be exposed to the allied spear —and would prove to be much less vulnerable than had been supposed. The last German laid down his arms on Cape Bon in Tunisia on 12 May, 1943; but Monte Cassino, a little to the north of Naples, was still in German hands twelve months later, barring the road to the Alps. In the exultant aftermath of El Alamein these disillusionments were still veiled by the future. Only slowly did the public grasp the truth that the North African victory contained, hidden among its laurels, a commitment, that it was shaping the war in a certain direction and that there would be no Second Front in 1943 any more than in 1942. War is like knitting: the task is apt to be resumed at the point at which it was dropped.

Churchill had imposed his ideas and his will upon more or less acquiescent, more or less reluctant, more or less protesting, allies. He had argued and manœuvred against them all; Stalin, Roosevelt, Marshall, Hopkins, Beaverbrook, the muttering, surly House of Commons, and the diligent, unpaid agents of the Kremlin chalking their slogans ("Britain blancoes while Russia fights") on factory walls. He had fended off the hands of the professionals of war, plotting in their lodges in the service clubs and the Parliamentary committee rooms, anxious to share with him the burden of strategy, prepared to wrest it from him when the time came. The time had not come.

In due course, Churchill's strategic directorate would

pass from his hands, not to a war cabinet, not, certainly, to Parliament, but to the new super-power, alone able to be master simultaneously on land, sea and air, supplied as she was by an industrial complex of giant strength, the United States. Britain had lost one war in France in 1940 and another in Malaya in the early weeks of 1942. Had lost them, and would survive. In a third struggle she could not prevail: the diplomatic, political struggle against the smiling power beyond the Atlantic, the good friend who was also the impatient heir. In due course, the United States would assert her right to shape the clay she furnished. But at the end of 1942, after eleven months of world-circling, and mainly catastrophic, events, after many and wearing challenges, the war was still Churchill's war, was stamped deeply with his imagination and bore his signature. The pattern had been set by him; the setback, for which also he would be responsible, still lay enshrouded by the future.

One day, in the early weeks of 1943, he was about to enter his aeroplane in Algiers for the hazardous flight back to England when a message was brought to him. An aircraft carrying others of his party had crashed; two brigadiers had been killed. Churchill paused for a moment, deep in melancholy thoughts. Then he said: "It would be a pity to go, with this mighty drama still unfolding. . . . But it's not so bad. It is a clear run-in from here." And he added, with a sudden grin: "Even the Cabinet could manage it."

Then he mounted the steps and the aircraft took off for home.

# Notes

**CHAPTER I:** *Porcupine Bank to Chesapeake Bay*

1. "Read this alone—and the war can be won"—pamphlet issued by Imperial Army Headquarters to the 25th Army.
2. Lord Halifax's Diary, 11 December, 1941.
3. Verbal communication.
4. J. R. Tournoux, *Pétain et de Gaulle*.
5. In the months that followed, Dill made a fine contribution to Anglo-American military collaboration.

**CHAPTER II:** *Lion in a den of Daniels*

1. Verbal communication.
2. The McGovern Paper.
3. Major-General Sir Edward L. Spears, *Assignment to Catastrophe*, vol. 1: *The Fall of France*, p. 215.
4. Winston S. Churchill, *The Second World War*, vol. 2, p. 183.

**CHAPTER III:** *The Christmas tree on the White House lawn*

1. *Op. cit.*, vol 2, p. 140.
2. M. M. Postan, *British War Production*, pp. 117, 176.
3. J. M. A. Gwyer and J. R. M. Butler, *Grand Strategy*, vol. 3, part 1, pp. 164–7.
4. Halifax Diary.

5. *Time*, 11 January, 1942.
6. *Time*, 26 January, 1942.
7. Halifax Diary, 27 December, 1941.
8. *The Times*, 16 January, 1942.


CHAPTER IV: *Forebodings*

1. A. J P. Taylor, *English History 1914–1945*.
2. Gwyer and Butler, *op. cit.*, pp. 246–7, 280.
3. Churchill, *op. cit.*, vol. 3, pp. 421–2.
4. *Op. cit.*, p. 422.
5. *The Rommel Papers*, ed. B. H. Liddell Hart, p. 95.
6. Maxime Weygand, *Recalled to Service*, p. 308.
7. The truth about Singapore seems to have been brought home to Churchill during the 1941–2 mission to Washington. "One day in the middle of January I found him in a positively spectacular temper. He had just learned from Wavell that the defences of Singapore were built only to meet attacks from the sea."—Lord Moran, *Winston Churchill*, p. 29.


CHAPTER V: *Advance from Moscow*

1. *The Economist*, 24 January, 1942.
2. *New Statesman*, 14 February, 1942.
3. *Forward*, 3 October, 1936.
4. William R. Rock, *Appeasement on Trial*, p. 323.
5. Gwyer and Butler, *op. cit.*, p. 81.
6. *Sunday Pictorial*, 19 January, 1942.
7. *Ibid.*, 26 January, 1942.


CHAPTER VI: *"Our duty to overthrow him"*

1. *New Statesman*, 24 January, 1942.
2. Letter to *The Times*, 26 January, 1942.

3. Sir John Kennedy, *The Business of War*.

4. Cecil Edwards, *Bruce of Melbourne: Man of Two Worlds*, p. 303.


CHAPTER VII: *Site for a Shinto shrine*

1. "The thrust of eighty or ninety millions of hardy war-like Asiatics."—Winston Churchill, House of Commons, 27 January, 1942.

2. "To fall in a hail of bullets is to meet a hero's death, but there is no glory in dying of disease"—the Japanese Army pamphlet quoted in note 1 to Chapter I.

3. *Sunday Express*, 8 April, 1934.

4. Kenneth Edwards, *Uneasy Oceans*.

5. Letter to *The Times*. 25 March, 1929.

6. *Daily Herald*, 7 May, 1930.

7. *The Times*, 5 February, 1938.

8. Vlieland Papers, King's College, London. C. A. Vlieland was Secretary of Defence, Malaya, 1938–45.

9. Viscount Slim, *Defeat into Victory*, p. 366.


CHAPTER VIII: *"The Government must break up"*

1. House of Commons, 20 May, 1942.

2. Halifax Diary, 15 August, 1941.

3. In conversation with Liddell Hart, 19 March, 1942.

4. *Time*, 23 February, 1942.

5. Halifax Diary, 15 August, 1941.

6. Halifax Diary, 11 April, 1942.

7. Kenneth Young.

8. *The Economist*, 7 February, 1942.

9. *The Spectator*, 13 February, 1942.

10. *Tribune*, 19 February, 1942.

11. *News Chronicle*, 24 February, 1942.

12. *The Eden Memoirs: The Reckoning*, entry for 18 February, 1942.

13. *The Goebbels Diaries*, p. 96 (entries for 18 and 21 February, 1942).

14. Lord Moran, *op. cit.*, p. 33.

15. *Ibid.*, p. 30.

16. Liddell Hart Archives: *Notes for History*, 18 March, 1942.

CHAPTER IX: *"I, Churchill, will serve you"*

1. *The Goebbels Diaries*, p. 130 (entry for 20 March, 1942).

2. The Gallup Poll showed that in February 1942 Churchill's leadership was approved by eighty per cent of the public.

3. Verbal communication from Lord Beaverbrook to the author, immediately after the event.

4. *World's Press News*.

5. Liddell Hart Archives: *Notes for History*, 19 March, 1942.

6. *New Statesman*, 21 March, 1942.

7. *The Times*, 13 March, 1942.

8. *The Economist*, 7 March, 1942.

9. Sir Arthur Bryant, *The Turn of the Tide*, p. 350.

10. *Ibid.*, p. 351.

CHAPTER X: *Stitching is not strategy*

1. Franklin D. Roosevelt Library, Hyde Park, New York.

2. "Aux Armes, Citoyens", *New Statesman*, 18 April, 1942.

3. Franklin D. Roosevelt Library, Hyde Park, New York.

4. *The Times*, 1 May, 1942.

5. Thus Owen repeated a phrase used by Beaverbrook in conversation with Lord Bruce of Melbourne in July 1942 (Edwards, *op. cit.*, p. 303).

6. Eric Sevareid. Columbia network, Washington commentator.

7. John Vandercook.

8. Cathryn Cravens. New York Station of WNEW

9. *New York Times*, 24 April, 1942.

10. *The Economist*, 21 May, 1942.

11. *Daily Herald*, 25 and 28 April, 1942.

12. *News Chronicle*, 28 April, 1942.

13. Robert E. Sherwood, *The White House Papers of Harry L. Hopkins*, vol. 2, p. 558.

14. *Sunday Times*, 9 August, 1942.

15. Churchill, *op. cit.*, vol. 4, pp. 314–5.

16. *Op. cit.*, vol. 4, p. 324.

17. *Time* magazine.

18. *New York Times*, 21 April, 1942.

CHAPTER XI: *A Government of youth*

1. *New Statesman*, 16 May, 1942.

2. James Leasor, *The Clock with Four Hands*, p. 176.

3. Churchill, *op. cit.*, vol. 3, p. 472.

4. *Op. cit.*, vol. 4, p. 375.

CHAPTER XII: *"The monstrous iteration of events"*

1. Political Correspondent, *Manchester Guardian*, 24 June, 1942.

2. London Correspondent, *New York Herald Tribune*.

3. Alan Bullock, *The Life and Times of Ernest Bevin*, vol. 2, p. 177.

4. Churchill, *op. cit.*, vol. 4, p. 390.

5. *News Chronicle*, 26 June, 1942.

6. *New Statesman*, 27 June, 1942.

7. *New Statesman*, 20 June, 1942.

8. *The Spectator*, 26 June, 1942.

9. Isaac Deutscher, *The Prophet Armed: Trotsky 1879–1921*, p. 482.

10. Napoleon, *Correspondence*, vol. II, p. 162.

CHAPTER XIII: *The thirteenth stroke of a crazy clock*

1. Churchill appointed Boothby to the Council of Europe in 1949 and recommended him for a K.B.E. in the Coronation Honours List. He did not, however, offer him a post when he returned to office in 1951.

2. Tournoux, *op. cit.*, p. 177.

CHAPTER XIV: *Mr. Churchill's Privy Council*

1. Military and Historical Journal: No. 10, 1966, Moscow. Zhukov's account of the Battle of Moscow. "Marshal Shaposhnikov, the Chief of Staff, said to me after the meeting: 'You were wrong to argue. The whole question had been settled by Stalin long before you arrived.' 'Then why ask our opinion?' I replied. 'I don't know, I don't know, my dear,' Shaposhnikov said with a heavy sigh."

"Greece was a political masterpiece; we succeeded in isolating that country. . . . Only the Italian army failed us completely"—Mussolini, reported in *Ciano's Diary*, p. 336.

Countless examples exist of Hitler's addiction to the same failing. One of the milder outbreaks occurred after Rommel had told him the position in North Africa was hopeless. "Hitler said that he was a defeatist and that he and his troops were cowards. Generals who had made the same sort of suggestion in Russia had been put up against the wall and shot." (Desmond Young, *Rommel*, p. 178.)

2. S. E. Morison, *Strategy and Compromise*.

3. Michael Foot, *Evening Standard*, 16 July, 1942.

4. *New Statesman*, 8 August, 1942.

5. *New Statesman*, 26 September, 1942.

6. Harold Laski, *New Statesman*, 26 September, 1942.

7. Foreword to Bagehot's *The English Constitution*, 1963.

8. House of Commons, 9 September, 1942.

9. *Reynolds News*, 7 June, 1942.

10. Lord Moran, *op. cit.*, p. 82.

11. *Ibid.*, p. 83.

12. *The Eden Memoirs: The Reckoning*.

13. Lord Alanbrooke, quoted by Lord Moran, *op. cit.*, p. 84.

### Epilogue

1. *The Economist*, 14 November, 1942.

# Bibliography

Bagehot, Walter. *The English Constitution*; foreword by R. H. S. Crossman. Cornell University Press, Ithaca, 1966.

Barnett, Correlli. *The Desert Generals*. Viking, New York, 1961.

Bryant, Arthur. *The Turn of the Tide, 1939–1943*. Doubleday, Garden City, 1957.

Bullock, Alan. *The Life and Times of Ernest Bevin*, Vol. 2. Heinemann, London, 1967.

Churchill, Winston S. *The Second World War*. 6 vols., Houghton Mifflin, Boston, 1948–54.

Ciano, Count. *Ciano's Diary, 1939–43*, ed. Hugh Gibson. Doubleday, Garden City, 1946.

Clark, Alan. *Barbarossa*. Morrow, New York, 1964.

Connell, John. *Wavell, Scholar and Soldier: to June 1941*. Collins, London, 1964.

Deutscher, Isaac. *The Prophet Armed: Trotsky 1879–1921*. O.U.P., New York, 1954.

Eden, Anthony. *The Reckoning*. Houghton Mifflin, Boston, 1965.

Edwards, Cecil. *Bruce of Melbourne: Man of Two Worlds*. Heinemann, London, 1965.

Edwards, Kenneth. *Uneasy Oceans*. Routledge, London, 1939.

Foot, Michael, *Aneurin Bevan,* vol. 1: *1897–1945*. Atheneum, New York, 1963.

Goebbels, Joseph. *The Goebbels Diaries.* Doubleday, Garden City, 1948.

Grenfell, Russell. *Main Fleet to Singapore.* Faber & Faber, London, 1951.

Gwyer, J. M. A., and Butler, J. R. M., *Grand Strategy,* vol. 3: *June 1941 to August 1942.* 2 parts, H.M.S.O., London, 1964.

Halifax, Lord. Diaries. In typescript. City Library, York.

Harding, Field-Marshal Lord. *Mediterranean Strategy, 1939–1945.* C.U.P., Cambridge, 1960.

Higgins, Trumbull. *Winston Churchill and the Second Front.* O.U.P., New York, 1957.

Hitler, Adolf. *Hitler's Table Talk, 1941–1944.* Weidenfeld & Nicolson, London, 1953.

Jacobsen, Hans Adolf, and Rohwer, Jürgen, eds. *Decisive Battles of World War II: the German View.* Putnam, New York, 1965.

Kennedy, John. *The Business of War.* Morrow, New York, 1958.

Leasor, James. *The Clock with Four Hands,* based on the experiences of General Sir Leslie Hollis. Reynal, New York, 1959.

Martienssen, Anthony. *Hitler and His Admirals.* Secker & Warburg, London, 1948.

Moran, Lord. *Churchill: Taken from the Diaries of Lord Moran.* Houghton Mifflin, Boston, 1966.

Morison, Samuel Eliot. *Strategy and Compromise.* Little Brown, Boston, 1958.

Playfair, Major-General I.S.O. *The Mediterranean and Middle East,* vols. 1 and 3. H.M.S.O., London, 1954–60.

Postan, M. M. *British War Production.* H.M.S.O. and Longmans, London, 1952.

Rock, William R. *Appeasement on Trial*. Archon, Hamden, Conn., 1966.

Rommel, Field-Marshal. *The Rommel Papers*; ed. B. H. Liddell Hart *et al*. Harcourt Brace, New York, 1953.

Sherwood, Robert E. *Roosevelt and Hopkins: An Intimate Study*. Harper, New York, 1948.

Shinwell, Emanuel. *Conflict without Malice*. Odhams, London, 1955.

Slim, William. *Defeat into Victory*. McKay, New York, 1961.

Spears, Sir Edward. *Assignment to Catastrophe,* vol. 1: *The Fall of France*. Hill and Wang, New York, 1955.

Taylor, A. J. P. *English History 1914–1945*. Clarendon Press, Oxford, 1965.

Tournoux, J. R. *Secrets d'Etat,* vol. 2: *Pétain et de Gaulle*. Plon, Paris, 1964.

Tsuji, Masanobu. *Singapore*. St. Martins, New York, 1961.

Vlieland, C. A. Papers. In typescript. King's College, London.

Weygand, Maxime. *Recalled to Service*. Doubleday, Garden City, 1952.

Winterton, Earl. *Orders of the Day,* Cassell, London, 1953.

Young, Desmond. *Rommell*. Harper, New York, 1951.

Young, Kenneth. *Churchill and Beaverbrook*. Heineman, New York, 1966.


Files of the following newspapers and periodicals: *Chicago Tribune, Daily Herald, Daily Mail, Daily Mirror, Daily Telegraph, Evening Standard, Manchester Guardian, News Chronicle, New York Herald Tribune, New York Times, The Observer, Reynolds News, The Times,*

*Washington Post, The Economist, New Statesman and Nation, Punch, Time Life, Tribune, World's Press News.*

*Parliamentary Debates* ("Hansard"): *House of Commons* and *House of Lords.* H.M.S.O., London, 1941–2.

# Index